Life After Death

Life

After Death
by S. Ralph Harlow

Para Research
Rockport
Massachusetts

Life After Death
by S. Ralph Harlow

Copyright © 1961 by Doubleday & Company, Inc.
Cover artwork copyright © 1982 Para Research, Inc.
Published by arrangement with Doubleday & Co., Inc.

Library of Congress Catalog Card Number: 61-6508
International Standard Book Number: 0-914918-40-0

Typeset in 10 pt. Paladium on Compugraphic 7500
Printed by Alpine Press, Inc.
on 55-pound Surtone II Antique
Typeset by Anne Drueding

Published by Para Research, Inc.
Whistlestop Mall
Rockport, Massachusetts 01966

Manufactured in the United States of America

First Printing, September 1982, 4,000 copies

Contents

Introduction

The possibility of a life after this one is a subject that has always fascinated me. Because of this curiosity, I devoured all the books on the subject. Some of these books seemed much better than others. When I first read Ralph Harlow's account, I found it to be as good as the best books I had read. And even more, it was well written and contained the depth of knowledge I had always wanted. To me, it reflected a long history of what life after death was all about.

Like everyone who reads a good book, I had to go out and tell all my friends about it. I found that others who read this book agreed with my conclusions and that it was held in high regard by those who had delved deeply into the subject. It just seemed I wasn't telling them anything new. By the time I read it, the book was a classic in the field. When I read it again, I realized that this book is particularly relevant now. In the last few years interest in life after death peaked because of the astounding scientific research and reporting of Elisabeth Kubler-Ross, Kenneth Ring and others. It is interesting to consider that their approach differs from the historical one which inspired the founders of both the British and American Societies for Psychical Research. These societies were founded to investigate life after death, but their investigations centered on mediums who said they could contact the dead.

The recent scientific investigations conducted by parapsychologists here and abroad have centered on the out-of-body experiences of many people who have come close to death and then recovered. The experiences of these astral travellers have a compelling similarity. They claim to have actually gone into a dimension of life and experience where they met and interacted with those who have died and other spiritual beings. They described the landscape in terms similar to the description in this book and their experiences have much in common with Ralph Harlow's account.

Although much of recent life after death research is still being hotly disputed, the results have been of great interest to the general public in their search for answers about a life after this one.

This current research shows much in common between people who have experienced these phenomena and the historic literature on the subject. That research also shows a correlation with spontaneous out-of-body experiences. Each of these people is convinced that they left their physical body and had an experience in another realm of being. These experiences have been called Astral Projections, Astral Travel and out-of-body experiences. Much has been written on these subjects and Brad Steiger has related Astral Projection to near death experience in his book, *Astral Projection*, published by Para Research, Inc. in 1982.

As readers, most of us want the material in a non-fiction book to be plausible and as objective as possible. But we also want more. We want the material to be easily read and understood, with a continuity that holds our interest and provides an enjoyable experience. This book becomes even more valuable because it is so well written and easily understood. Much credit for that must go to Evan Hill, head of the journalism department at the University of Connecticut and a well-known writer himself. Evan Hill was the actual writer of this book and he worked closely with Ralph Harlow on it to make the book well worth reading. Although Hill professes great skepticism about the possibility of life after death, he threw himself into the project of writing this book and remained faithful to Ralph Harlow's material.

When my eldest son attended the University of Connecticut, he studied journalism under Evan Hill and got to know the professor very well, causing me to feel an even greater kinship to this true classic.

Life After Death will make a great contribution to your experience and knowledge. This book will not only be enjoyable reading, but will also give you a deeper understanding of life after death and all the possibilities it holds for each of you. If there is an afterlife, and we all hope there is, it behooves all of us to be knowledgeable about this far country before we travel there.

Enid Hoffman

1

Out of the Darkness of Doubt

He was a tall handsome young man in his early twenties, wearing the uniform of a flyer and the silver wings of a pilot. On his left breast were combat decorations, and on the Pacific Theater ribbon were bronze battle stars.

As he came down the aisle of the crowded wartime train he looked at me, turned his head away, and then looked back again as if he thought he had seen me before.

"Is this seat taken?" he asked, and I shook my head.

He sat and we rode for some time in silence, traveling north out of New York City, heading toward Northampton and Smith College, where I was teaching religion and philosophy.

Then he asked, "Isn't your name Harlow? Don't you teach at Smith?" I nodded.

"I thought so," he said. "I want to thank you for something. Something quite important. Before the war I was a student at Williston Academy in Easthampton, and you came there to talk one night. I even remember the title of your talk—'Evidences for Immortality in Psychical Experiences.' " He laughed. "Quite a mouthful for a title and it sounded pretty dull. I only went out of curiosity. But I'm glad I went, more glad than you can know."

He paused, fumbling for words, trying to say exactly what he meant. "You told us about your own psychic experiences: about the time the inkwell cracked, and the figure you saw that night in Greece, and what was it—a vision—that you and Mrs. Harlow saw that time?

"I don't think you knew it—how could you?—but when I went into the lecture hall that night I was an atheist. Or if not, the closest thing to it. I had no belief in immortality and I had little faith in a personal God. Religion made no sense to me; it promised nothing and it certainly offered no evidence."

He looked past me out the window and then, as if speaking to himself, he said, "You know, when you fight a war you're supposed to be scared. You're alone. Oh, you have your crew and other aircraft around you on a bombing mission, but you're still alone, and you feel alone, and you know how much you depend on others—on your navigator, on your bombardier, on your gunners, and on the men on the ground who got you into the air and who will get you back on the ground. You have good reason to be scared."

Then he turned to me. "But, you know, I was never scared in combat. Not once. At Williston you recommended some books we might like to read on this business of personal survival. Well, I got some of them and I read them. I read more when I went to Yale, and by Pearl Harbor Day my whole outlook had changed. I don't know if you meant to have this happen to some of us but I haven't the slightest fear of death. I didn't when I was in combat. For I know that death is the surest hope of life." He grinned. "Sounds screwy, doesn't it?"

I shook my head and started to speak, but he interrupted. "Well, anyhow I'm grateful to you. I have what you ministers would call an enduring faith and you're responsible. I have wanted to thank you and now I have." Then he turned to the magazine in his lap, ending the conversation as if it somewhat embarrassed him to continue.

I did not tell this young man that his experience did not "sound screwy" or that it was not too unusual for persons with doubts to find faith by looking for evidence of survival—by opening their eyes with healthy skepticism to examine what we have learned to call paranormal or psychic experiences, those happenings which cannot be explained by scientific knowledge now in the hands of man.

In the last forty years I have given hundreds of public talks about psychic phenomena and their possible connection with a life after death. The subject seems irresistible to thinking adults. And indeed it should be, for we are hopelessly blind to our responsibilities as humans if we refuse to explore the unexplainable simply because we cannot explain it, or because we suspect the explanations might make us uncomfortable or will upset the laws of the universe as we now know them.

I can understand what happened to that young pilot when he began to see through previously closed doors after hearing my talk at Williston, for it was also a college professor who opened my eyes. In 1906, when I was a sophomore at Harvard, I was fortunate to be able to study under the great philosopher William James.

That year was Professor James's last at Harvard, and I took two courses from him: Psychology I and one on "The Varieties of Religious Experience." He was a man of towering intellect, calm, soft-spoken, and gentle. He had genuine humility and a wonderful sense of humor. He exuded greatness and we all felt it. His illustrations had great simplicity and clarity and they brought sharpness to the most complex subject.

I remember walking across Harvard Square with him one dismal November afternoon with the drizzle dampening his silver-gray hair and beard. I looked down into the gutter and saw the reflection of the street light in the muddy water. Because of the heavy daytime fog the reflection of the light was brighter to me than the light itself, and I said to Professor James, "If I did not know which was the real light I might have thought that the reflection was real and the real light was the reflection."

Professor James stopped and looked down at me for a moment. Then he smiled. "Yes," he said. "Now how do we know that what we observe around us, in what we call this physical universe, is really what it appears to be instead of the reflection of the mind of God? And that reality, as we shall come to know it, will be something else?"

That tall gentle philosopher and psychologist had a profound influence on me; it was he who excited my interest in psychic phenomena. He himself studied paranormal experiences and was a member of the Committee on Psychic Research, one of the earliest American groups to undertake serious investigation of the subject. And it was he who made me understand that unfamiliar concepts need not be dismissed merely because of their strangeness. Once after class he told me, "There is no pain in the world like the pain of a new idea." And I have learned, in the half century since his death, how accurate he was.

As a young college student I had the same doubts as the youth who had heard me at Williston. Although my father was an ordained minister and I was raised in a family with strong and genuine religious feeling, I walked into Harvard Yard as an agnostic. I could not believe on the basis of faith alone; I wanted proof, some external evidence that could give me strength in what I wanted to believe. My father's fundamentalism seemed too oversimplified, too dogmatic, too commanding. It gave him comfort, as it does to millions of Americans today, but it was not sufficient for me. As a boy Father had been a member of Henry Ward Beecher's liberal church, and though he had been influenced by Beecher's probing, inquiring mind it was Princeton College and its theological seminary, then a Calvinistic Presbyterian school, that left a deeper imprint on his thinking.

Father's religion was based on authority, and to him authority became truth. To other Christians who equate authority with truth, humans alone are not capable of struggling with the mysteries of life and death, of creation and ultimate goals; these mysteries are too baffling and far beyond the power of our feeble minds. The solutions are to be found only in divinely revealed authority, which once accepted must be taken with infinite trust and which in return promises security, peace, salvation—and freedom from further search.

Such authority may be the church, the Bible, or the sacred writings of prophets or saints. These authorities exist in the religion of the Moslems and in the religions of India and China as well as in Judaism and Christianity.

But, along with millions of other Christians, the single answer of black-and-white authority did not satisfy me. As George Eliot once wrote, "There are those of us...who must have our affections clad with knowledge."

And when I saw that the great mind of William James was unafraid of the unknown, undismayed by it, even curious about it in a time when psychic research was in disrepute and often compared to conjury and alchemy, I was encouraged to open up my mind and dare to see. I began to do what Julian Huxley, the great English biologist, recommended when he wrote, "Sit down before the fact as a little child; be prepared to give up every preconceived notion; follow humbly wherever and to whatever end nature leads, or you shall learn nothing. I have only begun to learn content and peace of mind since I resolved at all risks to do this."

Even in my early childhood I was exposed to events that I now know are psychic phenomena. Shortly before the birth of my sister Anna my mother experienced an apparition. She told us that one night she saw two "angelic forms" above her bed and they looked at her and smiled. Of course it is possible that this was a simple hallucination, but in the light of other experiences in my life I am unwilling to dismiss it so simply.

As Anna grew older she developed what was clearly a sensitivity to paranormal communication—she was clairvoyant and telepathic to some degree—but at first we considered these things as somewhat strange curiosities which were not worth much thought and which could be explained by coincidence or the quirks of memory.

Of course my father, as a minister, was exposed to reports of psychic phenomena and was often asked to explain them.

He admitted, as did my mother, that there was reality to these strange reports; that not all of them were hoaxes or frauds or the products of overactive imaginations. But in his fundamentalism he was positive that the genuine article was a visitation of the devil; to him such phenomena could be nothing else, and such experiences were to be avoided at all costs.

As I became more interested, not only researching into the thousands of volumes written in this field but also attending séances with some of the world's most reliable mediums, he at times became impatient and irritated with me. I remember one day when I described a particularly impressive sitting during which a medium had brought us several messages.

Father snorted. "When I want to talk to your mother after she dies," he said, "I do not propose to sit in a darkened room with someone in a cabinet and wait for a voice. If she wants to talk with me she can meet me in the open street or in church."

"On the other hand, Father," I replied, "when you are in Boston and you want to talk to mother now, you enter a small booth in South Station, drop a dime into a slot, and speak into a piece of rubber. You say, 'Canton 1896,' giving the machine the magic number, and then you stand there with an expectant look on your face until you say, 'Is that you, Carrie?' and then you enter into conversation. To anyone watching you who was not familiar with the telephone this would certainly be strange and suspicious behavior.

"Yet if you went out on the street or into church, as you say, and attempted to talk with mother without the telephone it would be equally suspicious behavior. You use that telephone booth and that piece of rubber and that dime and that magic number because you know if you observe certain laws you get certain results. Just so in psychic phenomena we have come to know that if we follow certain methods we get certain results."

Curiously enough there are many fine minds, men trained in scientific methods whose techniques could be so useful in psychic research, who admit the laws of chemistry and physics and mathematics but who refuse to believe that there might be yet undiscovered laws governing paranormal events. They would never attempt to develop camera film in broad daylight, for they know the laws governing the process; and they do not accuse photographers of charlatanry when they use a red light in processing one kind of film, green light in processing another, and no light in processing yet a different kind. They understand the laws involved, and they respect them and they get results.

Laws

Must understand the Laws and work within them to get results

It is interesting → to observe that scents who are the first to observe and acknowledge Laws pertaining to the physical — turn away from " " " other dimensions.

But when it comes to the unexplainable they seem to refuse to admit that there might be any laws at all. They want the phenomena to obey rules they make themselves. If you or I attempted to hatch eggs from a hen that had never been fertilized by a rooster, these men would look at us with pity and would explain to us the rules of genetics, telling us we must obey them. But when it comes to the paranormal they cast aside the laws of science and insist on playing alchemist.

Once a professor of biology, a brilliant man in his field, said to me, "When I can determine the exact conditions under which the phenomenon takes place, and control all the conditions of the event, then I might be willing to study this field. Until then I shall remain unconvinced."

Using an example from his own field of biology I replied, "Well, I have heard that these beautiful butterflies we see in the springtime really emerge from cocoons. This is very difficult to believe but I will be convinced if on the first day of December, on the north wall of the Science Building, you will produce a cocoon and at exactly noon cause a butterfly to emerge from it. If you can do this I will believe your story; if you cannot I refuse to accept it."

This of course is a ridiculously unscientific approach. It is like saying that because diamonds cannot be found in the grains of the sand at the seashore they therefore cannot be found and were never found in the gravels of South African rivers. No scientist worth his degrees would ever make such a statement about diamonds, or geology, or biology, but in considering psychic science the scientists seem to fall apart mentally and be unwilling to trust the discipline that has made possible great discoveries in other areas.

All throughout history brave men have dared venture down unknown and untried paths, and many of them have been ridiculed and persecuted; some were actually put to death. In 1790 Dr. Luigi Galvani, the great Italian scientist, was jeered by fellow scientists as the "frog's dancing master" after his startling experiments that discovered what is now known as galvanic current. He was treated with contempt and scorn but he replied calmly, "I know that I have discovered one of the greatest forces of nature." That force was dynamical electricity.

A few years later, in 1798, the third edition of the Encyclopaedia Britannica, the first to be published in this country, included an article on electricity. Written by one of the outstanding scientists of the period, the article is about twenty pages in length and is startlingly comprehensive for the time. But its conclusion is more startling than its completeness. The author wrote: "Electricity will never be of any practical value to

History is dotted with great men who were subjected to ... ridicule when they presented a new idea which was not common ... at the time but later improved ... Scientist ... 1790 discovered galvanic current ... Electricity.

...ilization. Doctors may help patients with rheumatism, but for the most
... it will be used by magicians to entertain people with parlor tricks."

And only a few months ago a prominent American psychologist *and*
...nowingly echoed that embarrassing eighteenth-century prophecy when *Dr Louis*
...old me his attitude about paranormal phenomena. He said, "I know this *Pasteur.*
...e field and it is nothing but a little bag of tricks." *the French scientist*

...Louis Pasteur, the great French founder of the science of bacteriology *who*
... discoverer of antitoxins, was denounced by the scientists of his day, *discovered*
...d doctors, clergy, and lawyers were among his fiercest opponents. It is *Antitoxins*
...ot difficult to compile a list of the scientific giants who have pioneered and *was*
...struggled with the pains of new ideas, accepting the taunts of their *denounced*
colleagues "till the multitude make virtue of the faith they had denied." *by everyone*

As in earlier, then primitive scientific fields, the area of psychic *including*
research was quickly populated with some of the great minds of our age. *the clergy*
My former professor, William James, was one of the founders of the *of his*
American Society of Psychical Research and was extremely active in the *day*
study of such phenomena. Sir William Crookes, the British physicist who *now we*
invented the Crookes tube that first emitted X rays, was once dropped as *know*
president of the Royal Academy of Science because he refused to give up his *how many*
studies of psychic phenomena. Lesser scientists were hostile to his studies of *lives the*
the paranormal and seemed to feel they would be contaminated by his *knowledge*
interests if he were not in some way condemned. Ten years after his *of bacteria*
dismissal by the Royal Academy he was re-elected president of the *has saved.*
Academy—because he was then Britain's greatest scientist.

At his second inauguration in Albert Memorial Hall in London he told
the world that his attitude about the paranormal had not changed. He said,
"There are many here tonight who believe that one reason I have been re-
elected president is because I have abandoned my studies in the field of
psychical phenomena. They should know that during the past ten years I
have continued these studies and am more convinced than ever of the
significance and importance of the facts discovered in this field."

The French astronomer Dr. Camille Flammarion, a member of the
French Academy of Science, was also an avid investigator of the
paranormal. He produced ten books on the subject, and his three volumes
on *Death and Its Mystery* is the largest collection of case studies in this field
that has yet been published. Sir Arthur Conan Doyle, the British physician
who turned novelist, is better known for his Sherlock Holmes than for his
extensive psychical research, but he was an extraordinarily enthusiastic and
convinced researcher into the paranormal. His countryman Sir Oliver
Lodge, however, became much better known for his conviction that the

dead may communicate with the living than for his great work in physics, electricity, and telegraphy.

In many respects research into the world of the unknown is still as unpopular as Columbus' belief that the world was round, but a healthy scientific attitude is beginning to combat it. At Duke University in North Carolina Dr. J. B. Rhine has been studying extrasensory perception (ESP) for more than thiry years, and his Parapsychology Laboratory has produced startling indications that the mind is more powerful—and more strange—than we have ever dreamed it could be.

Work is going on at Columbia University, as in the psychology departments of many American colleges, and recently Swarthmore College in Pennsylvania established a lectureship in psychical research. The strange, exciting, and uncomfortable world of the paranormal is achieving some status; many men of stature admit that their minds are not closed, and many are doing serious spadework in the area, looking for truth.

Many of them have come to the conclusion reached by the great American inventor Thomas A. Edison, whose twelve hundred patents— including the typewriter, the phonograph, the incandescent lamp, the electric locomotive, the railroad signal system, the motion-picture camera, the automobile starter, synthetic rubber—affect our everyday lives. Edison had no doubts about the value of psychic research.

Some years ago I became acquainted with his long-time associate, Dr. Miller Hutchinson, a man of no small ability himself, having been awarded the diploma of the International Academy of Letters and Science, the Cross of Honor for scientific and literary achievement, and a gold medal by Queen Victoria for "exceptional merit in the field of invention."

Once Dr. Hutchinson said to me, "Edison and I are convinced that in this field of psychical research will yet be discovered facts and data that will prove of greater significance to the thinking of the human race than all the inventions we have ever made in the field of electricity."

The crackpot, the mystic, the fundamentalist who needs to explain his world in the simplest terms—these people will always be with us. But Edison, Flammarion, Crookes, Rhine, Doyle, and Lodge do not seem to fit into these categories. We may be inclined to argue with ourselves and say, "Well, these men were certainly not naïve in their own fields, but in this other business—that of spirits and ghosts and mysterious messages from the other world—they are out of their fields. They are just as human and just as foolish as the rest of us. Isn't it possible that they could be brilliant experts in one area and utter crackpots in another?"

And of course this is possible. But in a field where so little is known that there are no experts who can qualify as an expert? Is it not sensible that if we accept the calm contributions of the scientifically trained mind in the fields of physics, biology, and chemisty—which in essence are just as mysterious to the layman as paranormal phenomena are to the scientific mind—that we should use the healthy skeptics in the world of physical science to explore the world of psychical science? Is it not as reasonable to respect Edison's convictions regarding psychical research as much as we respect his convictions concerning mechanical and chemical research?

Unless, of course, we do not really care about immortality or about the two great mysteries of mankind, the secrets of birth and death. And if this is the case we are indeed what the atheists claim that we are—nothing more than a temporary compound of chemicals: some calcium, some oxygen, some hydrogen and phosphates which function for some presently unknown reason ("But we'll find out one day"). And when these cease to function the compound sloughs itself back into the earth, eroding with the loam and the shale and the clay. And there is nothing more.

But I cannot believe this. My whole life has been predicated on something more; my occupation as a minister and as a college teacher of religion and philosophy has naturally urged me to probe more deeply into my wonderings than do most people. Yet after almost three-quarters of a century of life I do not know the answer.

Actually in many respects I am no farther along in my inquiries than I was a few decades ago when I stood in front of an ancient temple in Egypt and a companion translated a hieroglyphic inscription that had been carved into the stone long before the birth of Christ. The carving asked, "Who shall roll away the veil from the face of the ultimate mystery?" Beneath it an earlier tourist, a Greek of about two thousand years ago, had scratched, "Veil after veil has been rolled away, and still the mystery grows." And in many respects modern man is not much more enlightened about the ultimate mystery than were these two ancient writers.

But the mystery is still being probed, and is worth probing, for as Edison once said, "We know less than one millionth of one per cent about anything." And if knowledge for knowledge's sake is not reason enough for the probing, then we can concern ourselves with the thoughts of Ernest Renan, the great French historian and critic, who wrote, "The day when belief in an afterlife shall vanish from the earth will witness a terrific moral and spiritual decadence. There is no lever capable of raising the entire people if once they have lost their faith in the immortality of the spirit."

2

If We But Open Our Eyes

"But if these things really happen," my friends often ask me, "why have I never had what you call a psychic experience?"

Usually I reply, "You probably have and did not recognize it for what it was."

Even the most intelligent and the best-trained of us are remarkably ill-informed and poorly educated. The world contains such a mass of knowledge that we can never even hope to brush against all of it, let alone attempt to master it. And in so many areas we are hopelessly blind.

How many rich deposits of gold-bearing ore were ignored for centuries by countless thousands of men who saw them, perhaps fingered the quartz outcropping, and then passed on because they did not recognize what they had seen? How many of us have walked over mineral deposits or oil-rich land and seen only tall grass or scrub brush or "interesting rocks"? How many of us have ignored business opportunities simply because we did not perceive them until someone else, with brighter eyes and more perceptive mind, brought them to fruition while we watched and envied, saying to ourselves, "I saw it first, but I did not see it."

We have a habit of speaking of what we call the "lucky discoveries of science," and we tell stories about the laboratory worker who spilled a test tube and founded an industry. But we forget that countless humans had probably made that same error hundreds of times before yet had been unable to recognize what had happened.

The professional hunting guide finds game in the woods not because he has better eyes or ears but because he knows the significance of a sound or a broken twig or a musty smell. The professional woman shopper gets more value for her money because she is trained to recognize the strength of stitching, the toughness of beefsteak, the quality of the produce bins.

Who has not marveled at the weak-eyed bird watcher who sees the nuthatch when others cannot? Who has not marveled at the astronomer who on a clear night looks at the heavens with naked eyes and sees what we do not know enough to look for? Who has not felt slight shame after a walk in the woods with a wildflower hobbyist who has kept us from trampling the new violets of spring and has pointed out to us the checkerbloom, the columbine, and the pickerelweed?

We must be trained to see, and be willing to hear. As with the recognition of anything, our ability to recognize a psychic phenomenon depends on our understanding of the nature and the significance of the experience. At times the phenomena are so unspectacular that we dismiss them as simply strange or curious, and we forget them, not recognizing potential significance. We are like the hiker who saw the outcropping of gold quartz and called it "interesting rocks."

And then at other times the experience is so startling and extraordinary that we are filled with fear and awe, and the danger here is that our emotions begin to befog the evidence and we clutter it, obscuring it with what we think we heard or saw. We fail to record faithfully the happening, and the value of the experience to trained investigators begins to decline.

And there are times when we are deluded, sometimes unconsciously by ourselves, sometimes deliberately by charlatans playing on our emotions and our hopes.

Many if not most psychic phenomena are connected to the recent death of a relative or friend. When we lose someone who has been close to us it is natural for us to be upset and disturbed. Often we lose sight of our values; often we feel our faith slipping away from us; often we feel that God has cheated us and we cannot love a cheating God. It is then that we are more concerned with evidence of survival, more hopeful that such evidence exists, and less skeptical about it. We can become prey to our own hopes and to the frauds of the unprincipled.

If indeed we need trained guides to travel the spirit world, just as we need experienced woodsmen in the forests of Maine—and it would appear that frequently we do—then we must select our guides with extreme caution. There is no doubt that there have been hundreds of frauds perpetrated on innocent and naïve widows who cry for comfort after the death of husbands. Just as there are criminals who "salt" gold mines with shotgun blasts of pure gold so that they can sell stock, and just as there are confidence men who will sell you the Brooklyn Bridge or a gold brick if you are gullible enough, so, also, are there criminally minded "mystics" who will produce "evidence" of survival and messages from loved ones if we are gullible enough and if we pay them money. Psychic investigation, simply because it is so mysterious and strange, naturally lends itself to the skilled magician and the deliberate fraud.

And certainly there are times of desperation for even the most honest and dependable psychic medium. There are times when even the most gifted and genuine medium cannot bring in messages, just as there are times when our radio and television sets bring us only static. We do not condemn the entire electronics industry when our wireless communications are unreliable; instead we mutter about sunspots or bad reception and flick off the set until the atmosphere clears.

But when our previously dependable psychic communications develop static we are quite likely to doubt that we ever received reliable messages at all. It is then that the medium is tempted to resort to trickery, for the mediums want to be dependable and they do want not to disappoint. And even great scientists have not been beyond reproach in this respect.

I remember a story that William James once told us in class to illustrate this problem. He said that when he had been a medical student a biology researcher discovered that a frog's heart would continue to beat after it had been removed from the frog. Of course the Harvard Medical School faculty was fascinated by such a discovery, and James's anatomy instructor arranged to demonstrate the phenomena, with young James as assistant.

James prepared the demonstration, a simple experiment that had worked successfully hundreds of times. He removed the heart from the frog, placed a straw into it, positioned the straw and the heart on a stand behind a screen made of a white bed sheet, and played a beam of light onto the heart. The pulsing of the heart would be magnified by the straw, and the movement would be further magnified by the projection of its image on the screen.

And so on the evening of the demonstration, with a distinguished audience of surgeons and physicians—many of whom doubted that an excised heart would really continue to beat—listening to the lecturer and waiting for the demonstration, James noticed that the heart had ceased to beat.

"I knew what *should* happen," he told us. "And so I proceeded to reproduce the phenomenon."

He quickly tied a piece of fine silk thread to the base of the straw, and when his professor asked for the demonstration he adjusted the beam of light and tugged at the thread so that the straw acted as if the heart were still throbbing.

"Since that time," he told us, "I have had a certain sympathy with mediums who, when the psychic phenomena did not commence at a sitting, were tempted to reproduce it by trickery."

This illustration of course does not excuse trickery or fraud, for dishonesty is dishonesty regardless of its intent. But I hope that it will place some kinds of trickery into proper perspective. Because young William James hoaxed the Harvard Medical School faculty and his professor with a hidden silk string does not means that a frog's heart does not beat when removed from the body. All that we can say is that *that particular* demonstration was a fraud. We cannot say that the principle was disproved.

Thus it is with psychic research. We must be alert to discount and expose the hoaxes and frauds whatever their intent. And we must be equally careful not to be taken in by our hopes as they work on our subconscious mind. There seems to be incontrovertible evidence that there are genuine paranormal events, even though we cannot explain them.

It was James himself, admittedly baffled by his investigations after years of research and membership in the American Society for Psychical Research, who said in his Ingersoll lecture at Harvard, "As to the *reality* of psychic phenomena, which orthodox psychology scorns or ignores, I am not baffled at all, for I am fully convinced of it."

But how can we separate the hoax from the truth? The answer is as complex as it is simple: by being alert, skeptical, and persistent; by eliminating every possible logical explanation before even slightly leaning toward the paranormal; by using the same intelligent, searching turn of mind that has resulted in some of our greatest scientific discoveries.

One of the most commonly known psychic experiences was a frequent parlor game in the pre-TV era when American families did not gather in the living room to participate in the activity of group-staring. It is called table-tipping. Millions of Americans still toy with it, with varying success. The rules and equipment are simple, and if it produces results it often discovers latent psychic talent in a family, and probably leads to other experimentation.

In table-tipping a group gathers around a table, sitting comfortably, with their hands lying lightly on the table top and with each person contacting his neighbor by touching little fingers. Then a period of silence.

Sometimes there is long, unrewarding silence, and finally embarrassed failure and conceded defeat. But in a remarkably large number of cases, after a period of concentration and quiet, the table will actually tilt, raising two or more legs from the floor, and there are times when there is total levitation, with the table completely suspended in the air, unsupported, touched only by the hands of the sitters.

Sometimes there are rappings and knocks, and these unexplainable sounds are often interpreted as code messages from spirits. The code is quite simple. Each letter of the English alphabet is assigned a number: thus one rap means A, two raps mean B, five raps mean E, and so forth. Some groups become so skilled that they can ask questions aloud and the answers, purporting to come from the spirit world, are rapped back in reply.

During the beginners' adventure into the psychic world it is not difficult to discover who in the group has the greatest psychic power. By dropping one person from the group at a time it will soon become evident that the tapping, or table movement, is greater when a certain person is present, or is absent when he is not part of the group. By centering the experiments around this particularly sensitive or powerful person the psychic power seems to grow as the sittings continue.

Now, at this point, it is time to establish some basis for credibility.

Yes, it *is* possible that the table can be tipped by the knees of a practical-joking member of the group. Yes, it *is* true that trickery is made easier if such experiments are held in the dark, or in semidarkness, as many of them are. Yes, it *is* possible that the rappings can be made by the scraping of the creaking of a chair or by the leather heel of a member of the group. Yes, it *is* possible that a host can arrange entertainment for his guests by a few hours preparation with concealed mechanical or electrical devices. And mass hallucination cannot be ruled out as an explanation.

But I would be indeed naïve and credulous, or contemptuous of the intelligence of Americans, if I had not also doubted what we have seen and heard, and then eliminated the fraud. The reports of psychic experience included in this book have been filtered through the screens of logic, psychology, and the known laws of science. Wherever an experience was still vulnerable to the sentence that begins, "Yes, but . . ." it was eliminated. Only if the experience could not be explained—even partially—by trickery, hallucination, self-deception, coincidence, or science, and if the "Yes, buts" could not turn it into a mere interesting curiosity, was it considered a genuine, unexplainable psychic phenomena worth including in this book.

Only one doubt can remain, and the reader must be reminded of this doubt. That is the reliability of the investigator himself. Research can be no better than the researcher; the events recorded here can be no more accurate than the writer; and here of course I expose myself to attack. This is as it should be in any field of investigation, but although I admit my vulnerability I feel confident that my investigations have been sufficiently thorough and cautious to deserve an open-minded reading.

Now there is one more warning. This is to make clear the difference between spiritualism and psychic research. They are as different as astrology and astronomy, as alchemy and chemisty, and in my lectures on the paranormal I have always hoped that I have made this clear. Yet not long ago after a lecture I heard a lady in the audience cluck her tongue and say, "You know, really! I never knew that Dr. Harlow was a spiritualist!"

I am not a spiritualist; I am a Christian who is interested in and fascinated by what appears to be evidence that there is a world beyond the one we know, who feels that this is an unexplored world which might reward the researcher with new knowledge and that research might bear fruit. As a minister it is my job to be connected with any proof that the affirmations we make by faith are supported by facts.

Spiritualism is a form of belief that takes psychic phenomena and makes them the basis for religious belief. Although psychic experiences are given a prominent place in the Bible we also find fear and warning of spiritualism, for there is no substitute for the worship of the one true God. It was evident when the Bible was written, as it is today, that such a substitute would degrade the worship of God, for whenever a part is made the object of worship as a substitute for the whole it becomes idolatry. Spiritualism has made a religion out of psychic experiences, and this is a danger to high and pure religion. A picture, a shrine, an image in marble—these things may help remind us of our God, but when the symbol itself becomes the object of our worship and prayer, then we are idolatrous.

And now, having disposed of spiritualism and having laid a basis for credibility, we can turn to a series of psychic events that are as close to me as any such events can be. They involve my sister, the late Mrs. Anna Harlow Birge.

3

Through the Opened
Eyes of Anna

We were as close, Anna and I, as any brother and sister could be. She was two years younger than I, and our childhood friendship, although pocked with the normal sputtering of little spats and disagreements, actually grew stronger as we grew older.

We spent three years together in the same high school, and when I went on to Harvard she went to Wellesley College. When she married my close friend Kingsley Birge my wife and I worked closely with Kingsley and Anna in a New York City settlement house, for Kingsley was also a minister, and later we lived near each other when we both taught at International College in Smyrna, Turkey. When we returned to the United States both families settled in Northampton, Massachusetts, where I taught at Smith College.

Our summers were spent at the family place on Martha's Vineyard, a lovely island off Cape Cod, and the four Birge children and our own three youngsters frolicked on the beaches and explored the grassy fields together, closer in friendship than most cousins. It was a rare Thanksgiving or Christmas holiday that we did not share.

Now, fondness for a friend can dull our perception and make us less critical, and fondness for a blood relative who is also a friend can make us even more vulnerable in our judgments. But I do not think this is the case with my sister Anna. She was a calm, intelligent, well-informed woman whose mind had been strengthened by travel and by the occupation of her husband. No one who knew her could consider her even slightly neurotic or unstable or overly emotional. Her veracity was respected.

Therefore when she began to report her psychic experiences we regarded them as more important than the occasional remarkable coincidences that all of us have encountered. We knew that each Christmas Eve hundreds of thousands of children actually hear the tinkle of the sleigh bells hanging from the harness on Donder and Blitzen and hear the scrape of the sleigh on the roof. But we also knew that Anna was not a child; we knew that she was a perceptive, intelligent adult who was as familiar with hopeful hallucination as are the fond parents who smile at the reports of their wide-eyed, glowing children on Christmas morning.

But we could not explain what Anna saw, or what we saw and heard in her presence, or what purported to come through her after her death.

During Anna's life, for example, it was a constant source of amazement—and sometimes irritability—for us to observe what happened to the family phonograph when Anna was near. Anna could be seated at her desk, across the room from the phonograph, and the machine would begin to play. Yet it had not been switched on, had not been left switched on, and its playing arm had been left not on the recording but on its rest. Somehow the switch became engaged and the arm moved to the record. Many times her husband attempted to discover some rational explanation—the vibration of someone walking through the house, a child gleefully playing a trick on his mother, faulty mechanism in the phonograph. But he failed.

Once six of us were sitting before the blazing fireplace, chatting about the things that families discuss during long winter evenings. No one was in the next room, but the phonograph was there, and it began to play. It was a repetition of what had happened so many times before. Again we checked and found no normal explanation, and we never could explain it.

Anna's psychic sensitivity at table-tipping and with a Ouija board—a sheet of wood, lettered with the alphabet and numerals from 1 to 10, which spells out messages purporting to come from the spirit world when some persons lightly touch a wooden pointer—was equally unexplainable. But it was in what researchers call apparitions that Anna was most remarkable.

When Anna and her husband lived in Bristol, Connecticut, where Kingsley was minister of the Congregational Church, she was awakened one night by a touch on her hand. Kingsley was away at a conference in Boston, and Anna was alone in the house except for the children. Sleepily she groped for a child who had padded out of her room to join her mother, but felt nothing. Then, fully awake, she looked up to see her sister-in-law, Marguerite, Kingsley's sister, standing beside her bed. Then the vision vanished and she was alone in the room.

The next morning she received a telegram from Kingsley: MARGUERITE PASSED ON LAST NIGHT. GOING TO MAINE FOR FUNERAL. It was then that Anna remembered a pact that the six of us had made some years before—Anna and her husband, Kingsley; I and my wife, Marion; and Marguerite and her husband. All of us had been interested in evidence of survival, and, intrigued with Anna's apparent sensitivity to psychic phenomena, we had agreed that upon our deaths we would attempt to communicate with those of us who were still alive. And we had agreed that communication with Anna might be more easily accomplished because of her past experiences. I remember our conversation about acceptable evidence of survival— something that would eliminate subconscious memory of forgotten events or coincidence. I said, "It must be some sure signal of survival that could come only from the other world," and Anna nodded. "We must have clear-cut evidence," she said. "It must be clear-cut."

And now Anna had seemingly been contacted by Marguerite, only seconds after Marguerite's death and before Anna or her husband had been informed of their loss through conventional channels.

That afternoon, with the children all at school and the house quiet and empty, Anna strolled in the garden. She stroked the roses and pulled at the new weeds in the flower beds, and then felt an urge to look up at her second-story bedroom window. There, holding the white curtains aside, was Marguerite waving at Anna but remaining silent. Marguerite left the window and then reappeared, waving again, and three times this silent sequence was repeated, as if Marguerite were attempting to give sure evidence of her survival.

Is this the little child hearing sleigh bells on Christmas because he wants to believe in Santa Claus—or because he *does* believe in Santa Claus? Was this a hallucination or the attention-getting device of a lonely, neurotic woman? Those of us who knew Anna cannot think so, although at the time we all wished that the evidence had been more clear-cut, as Anna had wished when we had made our pact.

Once Anna and my wife, Marion, were shopping in downtown Boston, chatting and stopping to look into the huge display windows of the department stores. Suddenly Anna stopped and clutched at my wife's arm. "Marion," she said excitedly, "do you see that woman walking ahead of us? The one in black?" Marion nodded.

"Do you see the man walking beside her?"

"No, Anna. I see only her, walking alone."

"Oh," Anna said with some disappointment in Marion. Then quietly she said, "But he is there. It is a man from the spirit world. It is probably her husband who has just passed over." She turned to Marion again. "You can't see him?" Marion shook her head, and Anna said, "He has just turned to look at me and he seems to know that I am able to see him."

Anna died suddenly in 1925. She was buried in Bristol, and after the funeral services I returned to my office in Pierce Hall at Smith College. For the past several weeks one of my classes had been studying William James's *Varieties of Religious Experience*, a subject I had studied with James himself when I had been a student. That afternoon I had scheduled a conference with one of my honor students.

As we sat down at that big desk that warm October afternoon my mind was filled with Anna and with the words that had been spoken at the cemetery. I remembered James saying, "How native the sense of God's presence must be to certain minds," and I thought of Anna, and as I pondered I toyed with the thick, square glass inkwell that I had inherited with the office several years before. It was an empty, useless article since the invention of the fountain pen, but I kept it because it had a certain uncorrupted beauty about it and it served occasionally as a paperweight.

I slid the inkwell aside and turned to my student who sat quietly waiting for me to begin. "Perhaps," I said, "because I am just returned from a funeral we can approach the varieties of religious experience if I tell you something about the religious experiences of my sister Anna."

And then suddenly the inkwell split with a report like a revolver shot. It happened at the precise moment I spoke my sister's name, and we both stared at the fractured glass, still resting on the desk top where it had been before but was now cleaved cleanly in its center. There was no movement and the room was silent.

Then my student rose, trembling and unsure of herself. She was obviously greatly frightened. "What was that?" she gasped. "What was that?" She started toward the door. "I'm afraid, Dr. Harlow," she said. "I'm afraid to stay here."

"Don't be silly," I said. "You're a Smith senior and Smith seniors should not be superstitious. There's nothing to be afraid of."

"I don't care," she said. "I can't stay now. Can't I come back some other day? Please give me another appointment."

She was beyond comfort there in that room, and I must admit that I was not so calm as I wished to appear. I agreed to see her another day, walked her to the door, and returned to the desk and the inkwell. I carried it down the hall to the men's washroom and carefully washed it. There were no slivers, and the newly opened sides were as smooth as its polished exterior.

Back in my office I sat again at my desk, staring at the inkwell halves, attempting to reconstruct the last few minutes in exact detail. And then I heard a voice, sharply and distinctly. It said, "Is this clear-cut evidence?"

Next day I took the two pieces of glass to the science building and walked into the office of a colleague, a professor of physics. "Can you tell me how in the world this thing split the way it has?" I asked him.

He turned the pieces over in his hand, examining them carefully, and then he looked up at me. "Peculiar," he said. "I've never seen glass fracture like this. What'd you do? Strike it a hard blow with a very sharp instrument?"

I shook my head.

"A hammer?"

"No. I didn't touch it at all. I was sitting at my desk and it suddenly split, that's all. I was several feet away from it when it happened."

"Well," he murmured, "a sudden change in temperature might have done it. Did you open a window?"

"No. The window was closed. The door was closed. I would say the temperature didn't vary a fraction of a degree when it split."

"Curious, isn't it?" he said.

"Yes," I said. "That's why I'm here."

"Well, if what you say is accurate there's only one possible explanation for this type of fracture. And that is that some sudden vibration struck it. That could cause it to split. You know, something like a boat's whistle cracking a glacier."

I never told him the exact circumstances of the fracture, for I did not want to expose myself to his ridicule. And I never told him how significant his comment about vibration is to serious researchers in the psychic field. Again and again evidence has pointed to vibrations that have not yet been calibrated by known scientific methods, but if such vibrations do indeed exist man has not yet been able to document and prove them.

However, I left the inkwell with the physicist, for he asked if he could use it in his classes to demonstrate a peculiar fracture. A few years later I carried it to Duke University during one of my visits to Dr. Rhine at his Parapsychology Laboratories, and the fragments are there in his collection now.

Two weeks after Anna's death I went to visit my parents in Canton, Massachusetts, where Father was minister of the Congregational Church. We chatted for a while and then Mother said, "Ralph, I have something to show you. No, don't move. Just sit where you are."

She walked to her desk across the room and picked up a sheet of writing paper. She approached me and held it up. "Now tell me whose writing this is," she said.

The distance was too great for me to read the words, except with some difficulty, but I recognized the handwriting instantly.

"It's Anna's."

"So it seems to be," Mother said. "It certainly looks like it." Then she handed me the sheet.

It was a light gray page, with blue lines, and one edge was torn as if it had been ripped from a notebook of some kind. The message, in blue ink, was not parallel to the lines but had been written across them, and although it was punctuated correctly and was in itself a complete message it ended without a period.

It read:

> I cannot find words to express the joy and satisfaction of this work.
> We are busy every minute of the day and sometimes of the night too,
> but happy—oh, so happy! You [this word was underlined] must come
> and see for yourselves if you would be convinced. Do come, all [this
> word was triple-underlined] of you

"It's Anna's writing," I said. "And it has her words, her phrases, and even her habit of underlining." I looked up at Mother. "Where did you get it?"

"It happened three days ago," Mother said. "Father and I went to bed. We were alone in the house; we had no guests. Early in the morning, earlier than usual, I woke for some strange reason. And there it was on my bedside table. It was folded just once. That's all I know, except that I'm positive that it was not there when we turned out the lights. There was nothing on that table then, not a single thing. Father didn't put it there, I didn't put it there, and there was no one else in the house."

"There is no doubt about what it is," Father said to me. "But I'm sure you will disagree. We have different views on these things. It's supernatural, indeed it is, but it's not from Anna." And in Father's fundamentalism he found the answer. "This is an effort of evil spirits to mislead us. And don't be misled by them, Ralph."

I went upstairs to my parents' bedroom and looked at the bedside table. It was typical of New England, a carved walnut stand of the Victorian period. Its Vermont-marble top was smooth and cool to my touch as it had been since my childhood. There was nothing unique about it other than that for some strange reason the good people of the Deep South were beginning to regard such pieces as antiques and were paying ridiculous prices for them.

"And Ralph," Mother said as she stood beside me, "I've searched the house from attic to cellar to find other paper just like that sheet. There is none. No single sheets; no notebooks. And I cannot remember ever seeing any like it here."

I took the note with me when I returned home to Northampton and repeated what Mother had done with me. I held the unfolded note in front of Marion, who knew Anna's handwriting as well as she did mine, and asked her to identify it.

"Why, it's Anna's, of course," she said, quite matter-of-factly, not then knowing that the evidence gave strong indication that the note had been written by Anna after her death and had been mysteriously transported from some mysterious someplace to Mother's bedside table in a fashion unfathomable by modern man.

In the field of psychic research such an occurrence is called an apport, which means that a material object is moved from one place to another in a way that cannot be explained by physical force.

Anna's apport is not a singular experience; researchers have investigated and recorded thousands of such phenomena. But they have yet to produce a rational, acceptable explanation based on the laws of science as we know them.

In both of these phenomena—the incident of the inkwell and Anna's spoken words, and Anna's message—there are significant factors that indicate evidence of life after death. In the first place we know of Anna's psychic sensitivity during her life, and we know she had expressed a desire to give us proof of her survival after death. And we must remember the timing of the split inkwell: the fracture occurred at the precise moment I mentioned Anna's name. It did not split when I said "funeral," for there are many funerals; it did not split when I said "religious" or "experience" or "sister," for these would not be specific clues. But it did split when I said "Anna," for to me there was only one Anna, and only Anna had asked for "clear-cut evidence."

And Anna's voice asking, "Is this clear-cut evidence?" is especially significant if we will grant that I did not hallucinate this sentence. I admit there was no witness to this voice—and I do wish there were—but I'm not inclined to regard this experience as imagination. And certainly the split inkwell was not imagined. Not by my honors student, or my colleague in physics, or by Dr. Rhine at Duke.

To attribute the cracked inkwell to mathematical chance or coincidence requires more naïveté than I can muster. To do this would be to say that flat glass inkwells are subject to splitting while resting quietly, untouched on a flat-top oak desk, and that one inkwell in so many millions will fracture in such a manner. We would not care why that particular inkwell would split, but we would simply accept on faith that it would. And once we accept that mathematical possibility we would say that we can figure mathematically that one of these vulnerable inkwells will sit on the desk of a man with a sister named Anna, and that Anna would die, and that the man would speak Anna's name precisely at the time the inkwell split.

When we rephrase coincidence in such terms we see how nonsensical it seems. In fact, we would seem to be more naïve to accept coincidence as an explanation than to accept what these incidents purport to be—a contact with the dead. Perhaps both explanations are naïve, but certainly the psychic explanation is less so.

For me the most reasonable explanation is that, by means which I do not understand, my sister Anna was able to create a vibration that split the inkwell and that she did this for the explicit purpose of letting me know that death had not blotted out her conscious personality.

Regarding the apported note left on Mother's bedside table, I feel that the most reasonable explanation is that it is simply what it appeared to be—a message from Anna to her parents, left where they might find it. Certainly my parents did not play such jokes on each other, and they would not; the handwriting was definitely Anna's, and the contents of the note were typical of Anna—gay, enthusiastic, and delighted at being useful.

At times when I have discussed Anna with friends and then wandered into other similar experiences reported by reliable observers, someone has commented, "But does it not seem strange that if there *is* an afterlife, and if it *is* possible for us to communicate with the living after we are dead—does it not seem strange that so many of the messages are so trivial?"

One friend, a minister, said, "They seem to lack spiritual content. When there are so many important things we need to know, so many ethical points that need clarification, so much that humanity could gain from such contacts, we get the splitting of an inkwell and a message that leaves us with more questions than answers. We are tantalized and tempted to believe that this is proof, but we end up wondering why, if these spirits can indeed perform these miracles of communication, they do not give us something of value."

His point is well taken. I have often pondered this myself and I am not too satisfied with the results of my ponderings. Perhaps these really are insignificant contacts, but if they are contacts at all, however insignificant, and through them we touch the borders of the world of spirits, then they have amazing significance. They are evidence that we are not mere creatures of chance but that we come forth from the living God, born of His spirit, and that to Him we return. We shall have established eternity.

And I wonder if we really know what is significant and what is not. For we have often labeled great discoveries as trivia, and have mistaken the trivial for great new principles. In 1752 we called Dr. Franklin's kite experiment a curiosity, for we did not have the perception he had when he saw the world's first hot-air ballon ascend into the skies near Paris. At that time a French witness turned to Franklin, shrugged his shoulders, and asked, "But what good is it?" And Franklin replied, "What good is a newborn babe?"

Was it trivial when in 1860 in Frankfurt the German physicist Philipp Reis toyed with membranes, magnets, and electricity and discovered that sound could cause pulsations to travel along a wire? He recognized the principle of the telephone, which later allowed Alexander Graham Bell to toy with other "trivia" and give us a device that is so important to our daily lives that we take it for granted—and actually give it the status of a triviality.

Few great new inventions, especially those which at the time seemed to contradict tradition, have escaped scorn and ridicule from those whom we might expect to welcome such discoveries. When Edison's phonograph was first brought into the meeting of the French Academy of Science several members rose and left the room in disgust after hearing the first demonstration. One scientist exclaimed, "How can you sit here and be made fools of by this trickery?"

But not all members of the French Academy were as sensitive, or as shortsighted. The astronomer Camille Flammarion's studies in psychic phenomena convinced him that there is a life after death, and in his volumes of case histories are many glass-breaking incidents which took place at the time of death or immediately thereafter and are somewhat similar to my experience with Anna and the inkwell. (And it is curious that Flammarion estimates that more than 85 per cent of the recorded psychic manifestations appear to be related to some person who had died recently.)

One of my favorite Flammarion cases concerns a doctor, his sister, and an aging retired army captain who frequently dined together in the doctor's home in Marseilles. All three were agnostics; none could believe in immortality, and each strongly disbelieved that there could be any life after death.

One evening when they were discussing this subject the doctor said, "But we could be wrong, you know. And just in case we are what do you say that the first one who dies makes an attempt to contact, and convince, the survivors of our error?"

"Agreed," the captain said. "And because I am the oldest I am most likely to be the first one to be able to send such a message. What sign would you like me to give?"

They looked about the dining room, searching for some object that would seem possible for spirit communication and yet could not be influenced by normal causes. The doctor's sister pointed to the gaslighted chandelier above the dining table. A metal pipe attached it to the ceiling, and approximately halfway up the pipe was an ornamental glass ball.

"Can you rap on that?" the doctor's sister asked, most facetiously.

The captain laughed. "If you hear from me when I am dead I will be tapping on that pipe."

Not long afterward the captain left Marseilles to live in Palermo. The doctor and his sister quickly forgot the conversation, and they lost contact with their old friend.

About a year after the captain had moved away the brother and sister were dining in the same room where they had made the pact with the captain, and just before the meal was finished they heard tapping on the metal rod over the table. There were only a few taps and then the sound ceased.

As the doctor reported the case to Flammarion neither he nor his sister thought of the captain's promise at the time. They both thought the tapping was a curious event but about as important as the creaking of a house in a quiet night.

But the next evening at dinner the tapping occurred again. This time the doctor was intrigued enough to climb onto a chair so that he could feel the pipe. He had no other thought than that the tappings were the result of some natural cause, and he suspected that the pipe might have become hot from the gas jets. But it had not; it was cold.

On the third night the taps were much louder, much more persistent, almost expressing irritation. They ended suddenly with a sharp report and the ornamental glass ball suddenly split, with one half remaining on the pipe and the other half dropping to the center of the table.

It was then that the doctor remembered the pact they had made with the captain. However, they had no knowledge that the captain had died, so the next day the doctor wrote to Palermo, inquiring after their old friend. The reply told them that the captain had died in Palermo the day before the first tapping in their dining room.

According to Flammarion, the breaking of glass in connection with recent death is a fairly frequent psychic phenomenon. And my friend Wainwright Evans writes me of two other such experiences, one of them very similar to that of Anna and the inkwell.

He tells me that shortly after a friend had been killed in an automobile accident his family was gathered around a large table on which stood a heavy glass paperweight that had been around the house for more than twenty years. As the dead man's sister mentioned his name the glass paperweight split down its center.

The other incident concerned the family gathering after the death of a friend's father. The family was in the living room; the body of the father lay in the next room. In the silence of sadness a son said, "Let's have a drink," and his sister, shocked at what she considered a lack of respect, said indignantly, "How can you? Here Father lies in his coffin in the next room and you talk of having a drink!"

The brother started to apologize, but just then they all heard a sharp, snicking sound and they turned to look at the sideboard. There a sherry decanter had just split completely around its base, and the wine was spilling across the polished surface.

Later a son said, "If you had known my father you would have realized that he really wanted us to have some wine."

I cannot explain why so many of the recorded cases of paranormal experience involve the breaking of glass, unless there is indeed merit to the vibration explanation which my Smith colleague offered at the time of Anna and the inkwell. Perhaps persons who have passed over, or some of them, have access to an energy source that we have not yet discovered; perhaps this energy can be transformed into vibrations of a certain pitch that makes glass vulnerable to it.

But even tentatively to offer vibrations as a possible explanation seems to be putting such experiences out of their proper perspective. When I am tempted to make these things into black and white I remember the words of the great Episcopal preacher Bishop Phillips Brooks:

"This is what you are to teach your child; this is what you are to hold fast to yourself—*the sympathy and companionship of the unseen worlds.*

No doubt it is best for us now that they should be unseen. It cultivates in us that higher perception that we call 'faith,' which is as truly perception as is the sight of the eyes. But who can say that the time will not come when, even to those who live here upon earth, the unseen worlds shall no longer be unseen? In all times there have been men, who, at special moments, have seemed to see beyond the ordinary bounds of sense and actually with their eyes to behold forms of beings who belonged not to the earth but to the heavens. Who can say that some day, centuries off, when the old world shall be far older still, and shall have been purified by vastly more of pain and labor, it may not be given to men to see these beings of other worlds than ours, who even now, are around us, and who, we know, are living and seeking the same righteousness with us?"

It was St. Paul (II Corinthians 4:18) who said, "we look not to the things which are seen but to the things which are unseen; for the things which are seen are transient, but the things which are unseen are eternal."

4

The Six Angels
of Ballardvale

It was a glorious spring morning and we were walking, Marion and I, through the newly budded birches and maples near Ballardvale, Massachusetts.

The little path was spongy to our steps, and we held hands with the sheer delight of the day and the sheer delight of life as we strolled near a lovely brook. It was May, and because it was the examination reading period for students at Smith College we were able to get away for a few days to visit Marion's parents.

We frequently took walks in the country, and we especially loved the spring after a hard New England winter, for it is then that the fields and the woods are radiant and calm yet show new life bursting from the earth. This day we were especially happy and peaceful; we chatted sporadically, with great gaps of satisfying silence between our sentences.

Then from behind us we heard the murmur of muted voices in the distance, and I said to Marion, "We have company in the woods this morning."

Marion nodded and turned to look. We saw nothing, but the voices were coming nearer—at a faster pace than we were walking, and we knew that the strangers would soon overtake us. Then we perceived that the sounds were not only behind us but above us, and we looked up.

How can I describe what we felt? Is it possible to tell of the surge of exaltation that ran through us? Is it possible to record this phenomenon in objective accuracy and yet be credible?

For about ten feet above us, and slightly to our left, was a floating group of spirits—of angels—of glorious, beautiful creatures that glowed with spiritual beauty. We stopped and stared as they passed above us.

There were six of them, young beautiful women dressed in flowing white garments and engaged in earnest conversation. If they were aware of our existence they gave no indication of it. Their faces were perfectly clear to us, and one woman, slightly older than the rest, was especially beautiful. Her dark hair was pulled back in what today we would call a ponytail, and although I cannot say it was bound at the back of her head it appeared to be. She was talking intently to a younger spirit whose back was toward us and who looked up into the face of the woman who was talking.

Neither Marion nor I could understand their words although their voices were clearly heard. The sound was somewhat like hearing but being unable to understand a group of people talking outside a house with all the windows and doors shut.

They seemed to float past us, and their graceful motion seemed natural—as gentle and peaceful as the morning itself. As they passed, their conversation grew fainter and fainter until it faded out entirely, and we stood transfixed on the spot, still holding hands and still with the vision before our eyes.

It would be understatement to say that we were astounded. Then we looked at each other, each wondering if the other had also seen.

"Come," I said, and I led her to a fallen birch. We sat and I said, "Now Marion, what did you see? Tell me exactly, in precise detail. And tell me what you heard."

She knew my intent—to test my own eyes and ears; to see if I had been the victim of hallucination or imagination. And her reply was identical in every respect to what my own senses had reported to me. When she had finished she answered my unasked question.

"It seems to me," she said calmly, "that for those split seconds the veil between our world and the spirit world was lifted and for some reason, unknown to us, we were permitted to see and to hear what generally our physical eyes and ears are unable to sense."

Under normal circumstances, but probably only in subjects other than this one, I am considered a faithful, reliable witness. Attorneys have solicited my testimony, and I have testified in the courts, regarded by judge and jury as dependable and honest. And I record this story with the same faithfulness and respect for truth and accuracy as I would tell it on the witness stand. But even as I record it I know how incredible it sounds.

But I detest fooling myself or others in a matter which seems to me to have such significance for those of us who agree with St. Paul, "There are celestial bodies and there are terrestial bodies; but the glory of the celestial is one, and the glory of the terrestial is another." (I Corinthians: 15:40)

This experience of almost thirty years ago has greatly altered my thinking. Once both Marion and I were somewhat skeptical about the absolute accuracy of the details at the birth of Christ. The story, as recorded by St. Luke (Luke II 8-18), tells of an angel appearing to "country shepherds abiding in the field" and after the shepherds had been told that Christ had been born, "suddenly there was with the angel a multitude of the heavenly host praising God, and saying, 'Glory to God in the highest, and on earth peace among men with whom He is well pleased.' "

Our hymns and especially our Christmas carols contain some of the glory of the visitation of angels to the shepherds, and for years I wondered if the story from Luke was accurate reporting or if it was legend based on fantasy. Today, after that experience of the six angels at Ballardvale, Marion and I are no longer so skeptical. We believe that in back of that story recorded by St. Luke may well lie a genuine, objective experience told in wonder by those who had the experience.

As a child I accepted the angels in Luke as literal heavenly personages; then I went through a period when I felt that they were symbols injected into stories of imagination. Now, since Ballardvale, I no longer doubt that there may well have been an experience in which angel visitors were seen and heard. I cannot be dogmatic about it, as is the fundamentalist in his strong belief, or as is the materialistic psychologist who is equally dogmatic in denying it.

And Marion and I are less critical of our Roman Catholic friends and their beliefs about the visions at Lourdes. If we doubt that in 1858 a little fourteen-year-old peasant girl saw a "most beautiful lady" in a Pyrenees grotto, we must cast equally strong doubts about our own vision at Ballardvale. And we cannot; we have no doubts about what we saw.

But we must admit a certain reserve and caution in telling this story to others, for we frequently meet incredulity, an unwillingness to accept our testimony, and even ridicule. In a broad perspective this attitude is understandable, and we should be tolerant of it, but it is difficult to accept the scorn of educated persons whose minds are, but should not be, snapped shut against possible evidence of life after death.

Not long after the Ballardvale experience Marion and I attended a religious education conference of Sunday-school leaders and teachers at the University of New Hampshire. One noon, during our lunch hour with several other ministers, the conversation turned to the problem of immortality, which had been discussed in some of the classes that morning, and Marion had the courage to tell of our experience. The luncheon group listened, at first with excited interest and then with strained politeness. Finally one minister, unable to conceal his contempt, snorted, "It must have been a flock of bees!"

I thought of the French scientists leaving the demonstration of Edison's phonograph and branding it as a hoax, and I wondered if we really could accomplish anything by telling others of our experience. But then I thought about this man's occupation and I asked him, "What do you preach about on Easter Sunday?" He did not reply.

The apparition of the angels was our second experience with this type of psychical phenomenon. The first occurred when we saw what seemed to be Savas Ayerigdes—then five years in his grave—one early August night in Smyrna, Turkey, where I was teaching at International College.

We first met Savas in Smyrna during World War I, but before the United States became involved. It was because of his freshman grades that I sought him out and found that he lived alone on the edge of the campus in a windowless mud hut with a dirt floor. As usual, after year-end grades had been recorded, the faculty had met to discuss the progress of students. The name of Savas Ayerigdes dominated the discussion, not only because he held the highest grades of anyone then in the college but because those grades were higher than any student had earned in years.

I went to see him with the teacher's natural desire to meet an exceptional student. He was seventeen years old, a short, husky, black-eyed Greek, and fiercely intelligent. An orphan, he lived alone in Spartan simplicity in his one-room hut, and when he was not in class or studying he worked for nearby farmers to keep himself alive. The world had been harsh with him, and his religious views reflected this harshness; he was a complete and dedicated intellectual atheist.

Once he told me and Marion, "You know, if there is a God He must be a very cruel God to tolerate the cruelty there is in the world."

Marion and I grew very fond of him, and he was a guest in our house many times. Although his parents had been Greek Christians he was puzzled by our devotion to Christ. "My parents were ignorant," he said, "and their faith was blind. But you people are educated and yet you, too, are religious." Often he helped us put our four-year-old son John to bed and listened with intense interest while little John said his bedtime prayers.

One night when John was saying, ". . . and God bless Mommy and God bless Daddy," he opened his eyes, looked at Savas with the wonderfully uncomplicated honesty of children, and added, "and God bless Savas."

This was the beginning of the end for Savas' critical atheism. From complete nonbelief he came into a strong Christian faith and was later elected president of the college Christian Association. Then he became old enough to be drafted into the Turkish army, which at the time was trying to stop the British General E. H. H. Allenby in his surge up from Egypt to drive the Turks out of Palestine.

Before he left for the army we met Savas for prayer near a little olive grove on the campus. Not much later we received word that he had been killed in battle with Allenby's forces just outside Jerusalem.

But now, on that August night of the apparition, Savas was not in our minds. Little John was critically ill, so sick that we despaired for his life and had been given permission to return to America where he could get skilled treatment.

We walked toward the olive grove where Savas and Marion and I had prayed before he had become a soldier, and in the darkness Marion suddenly clutched at my arm. "Look!" she said.

About ten feet in front of us, with a suddenness that was almost electric, appeared a radiant, shimmering white figure. It seemed to emerge from the ground, and although it had the general outline and size of an adult human it lacked detail; we could not see hands or feet. We said nothing, and for possibly the span of two minutes we stood still, facing the luminous form, and it was as quiet as we. We heard nothing but we were filled with elation. Then suddenly the white form vanished as if a switch had been swiftly disconnected.

Marion and I sat down in the grove and discussed what we had seen. We could think of no natural explanation for what we had seen. But because it had occurred on the spot where the three of us had met for prayer we naturally associated the vision with Savas, and with some possible desire by our dead friend to give us comfort in our worries.

"It was little John's prayer that started Savas into Christianity," I told Marion. "Perhaps it may be that now John is going to leave us, and. . ."

It seemed possible to us then, and it does to us today, that we had been given this witness that the world of immortality is nearer than we are able to perceive with our physical senses. It may be that in our hour of need Savas had been able to give us this assurance that whether in life or death "underneath are the everlasting arms." (Deuteronomy 33:27)

We never had contact with Savas again, nor with what we might have suspected as Savas; but John is still with us. He did not die as we feared. In Boston he began treatment that ultimately restored his health, and today he is married and living happily in Iowa City, where he is on the faculty of the University of Iowa.

Few psychic phenomena are as striking as are apparitions, but one paranormal experience that took place on Martha's Vineyard during a spring college vacation was about as satisfying and comforting as any we have had.

Helen had come to me shortly after we arrived on the island, walking from her cottage to ours across back yards, and she told me then, with little emotion and great calmness, that she was dying of cancer. With death facing her, she was less casual now about my interest in proof of life after death. That spring and during the early summer when we returned to the island Helen and I held several long conversations about survival. They seemed to give her some comfort.

To Marion and to me, Helen was a very close friend; she was intelligent and stimulating, and two of her daughters had been students of mine at Smith. To our ten-year-old daughter, Betty, Helen was "Aunt Helen"—a really very dear friend.

Now young Betty was intelligently aware of the field of psychic phenomena in the same way the daughter of a marine biologist may well be aware that a moon jellyfish is an *Aurelia aurita* and that a starfish is *Asterias vulgaris*. She had not the psychic sensitivity of my sister Anna and had never experienced any paranormal phenomena, although she had heard her mother and me talk about them.

On the July afternoon when Helen died, Betty was at the beach a mile away, swimming with her cousin. Unexpectedly she appeared at the cottage on her bicycle, ran into the house, and asked her mother, "Has Aunt Helen died?" We did not know, but we asked her the reason for her question.

"No reason, I guess. Not really," she replied, somewhat bewildered by her own feelings. "I was swimming and just playing around on the beach and suddenly I knew that Aunt Helen was dead. So I came home to find out. Is she?"

We inquired and found that Helen had died while Betty was playing at the beach. This was Betty's first and only psychic experience.

But that night Marion and I experienced a strange event that amazed and delighted us because we felt quite strongly that Helen had contacted us.

We had been asleep for several hours when we were awakened by a beam of light on the bedroom wall. I got up and went to a head-high shelf on the wall. There, burning brightly, was an old two-cell flashlight which I had abandoned as useless almost two months before. Its batteries had corroded during the cold, damp winter when the house had been closed, and its switch was stiff and rusty. With some disgust I had shoved it back on the shelf, after my efforts had failed to achieve a glimmer, and I had promised myself to buy replacement batteries. But I hadn't and neither had Marion.

Yet now it was ablaze with light. It had not been burning when we turned off the lights before going to sleep, and no one had touched it since then. I switched the beam around the room, lighted up Marion as she sat in bed, and then turned off the stiff switch.

"Why did you turn it off?" Marion asked.

"Why not?" I asked. "It never works when you want it to, and then suddenly it wakes you up in the middle of the night. Working fine now." And I thumbed the switch back to the "on" position. But it was a dead. It would not light. I shook it and flicked the switch back and forth. I was wasting time.

"Marion," I said, "turn on the bedside light, will you?"

And I sat on the edge of the bed at one o'clock in the morning to examine that flashlight. I unscrewed the rusted bottom and removed the batteries; I examined the tiny bulb and reseated it more securely; I scraped the contacts to be sure they were clean. But it would not light.

Then Marion asked, "Did you try to get a message to Helen tonight?"

I nodded, and she knew what I meant, for both of us were familiar with the technique of mental communication, and occasionally we had achieved results with our attempts. That night before going to sleep I had attempted to send my thoughts into space, saying, "Helen, if you can give us any sign of your conscious survival won't you please do so?" And at one o'clock the battered flashlight had turned itself on. I replaced it on the shelf and we went to sleep.

As we went to bed the following night we again attempted to get light from the torch. But it was useless, and I placed it once more on the shelf. Before sleeping we both concentrated on contacting Helen and asked her to again give us a signal. At about two o'clock the flashlight woke us again; this time it was much brighter than the previous night, and throughout that summer and on into the winter that flashlight continued to function, producing unusually brilliant power, as if its batteries had been given an extra charge of electric energy.

The next afternoon I conducted Helen's funeral service, and as I stood by her casket, reading from St. Paul, there came over me a thrilling conviction that Helen was released from her frail and pain-stricken flesh and had gone into a new life, conscious and retaining the power of thought and action. I got new and vigorous meaning from the words of the service:

"It is sown in corruption, it is raised in incorruption; it is sown in dishonor; it is raised in glory; it is sown in weakness; it is raised in power; it is sown an earthly body; it is raised a spiritual body. There is an earthly body, and there is a spiritual body.... And as we have borne the image of the earthly, we shall also bear the image of the heavenly.... For this corruptible must put on incorruption, and this mortal shall put on immortality." (I Corinthians 15:42-4; 49; 53)

I closed the service, as I always do, with that beautiful prayer of Cardinal Newman's:

> O Lord, support us all the day long of this troublous life,
> Until the shadow lengthen, and the evening comes,
> And the busy world is hushed, and the fever of life is over,
> And our work is done.
> Then, of Thy great mercy, grant us safe lodging and a holy rest,
> And peace at the last; through Jesus Christ, our Lord. Amen.

I suppose that there are those who would insist that the flashing of the stubborn light was pure coincidence, or perhaps due to causes that we may not understand at present, but certainly not related to Helen's continued consciousness.

Perhaps they are right. But there seems to be an intellectual danger in using coincidence to tidy up our doubts in much the same way as we use a feather duster to redistribute the dust in a room and to ease our conscience. The room is no cleaner, but we feel that it is. There is a certain comforting tidiness about coincidence; it gives us a labeled box in which to conceal the experiences we are unwilling to sort out into their proper containers; it is like the New England farmer's culch pile; as long as it remains there in the attic with its assortment of picture frames, old books and love letters, a boy's first stamp collection, and broken chairs intended to be mended years ago, it requires no further attention. The fact that it exists is comforting enough, for there, piled up and out of sight, are the good intentions of a lifetime, and they have been as neatly disposed of as if we had accomplished them.

In the case of Helen and the flashlight, coincidence does not convince me. It may be tempting as an easy explanation, but it seems too easy. Chance does not explain this phenomenon so convincingly as does the possibility that Helen was its source.

And often when I ponder over those two nights, wondering if there could actually be a mechanical explanation, I remind myself of the words of Professor Alfred North Whitehead, the Harvard mathematician and philosopher, who said, "What is the sense of talking about mechanical explanations, when you do not know what you mean by mechanics?"

5

Margery

The Margery mediumship started with an atheist's conversion and a wife's irritation with her husband's new hobby.

Margery Crandon, an alert, vigorous, intelligent young woman set out to "fix her husband" one morning because her initial amusement with his interest in the paranormal had turned sour. She thought his viewpoint was simply ridiculous and was determined to prove it. She failed, but she started a chain of events that eventually resulted in some of the most startling psychic experiences on record.

Margery Crandon was the wife of Dr. L. R. G. Crandon, a famous Boston surgeon who was for almost two decades a professor of surgery at Harvard University Medical School.

The Crandons lived in a three-story brick house at 10 Lime Street, at the foot of Beacon Hill, in one of the most exclusive and oldest sections of Boston. Their home revealed their cultural and intellectual interests. Their library was large and extensive, and Roy Crandon had indulged himself in his fascination with Abraham Lincoln. His private collection of Lincolniana was superb, one of the finest I have ever seen, with its marble and bronze busts, photographs, papers, and biographies. He was respected as a Lincoln scholar. He was a Harvard graduate of fourteen years earlier than I, and had received both his master's degree and his medical degree from Harvard.

Although both his wife and his mother-in-law were deeply religious and had been active in the Congregational Church and in the City

Missionary Society, Dr. Crandon was an atheist. Once, when we were talking about the days before Margery's discovery, he told me, "I couldn't believe. I had cut up so many dead bodies and had never found a place where a soul might have been."

I replied, "We don't *have* souls; we *are* souls, living for a time in a physical body." And he then agreed with me.

But while Dr. Crandon was still an atheist, the great English physicist Sir Oliver Lodge came to this country to lecture about life after death, and Dr. Crandon went to hear him. When he heard Lodge voice his conviction that man is immortal, Dr. Crandon was puzzled. Lodge was an eminent scientist; his discoveries in the field of electricity had advanced civilization by decades; he was certainly not naïve or unaware of the rules for scientific research. Yet, as Dr. Crandon recalled to me, here was Lodge, the scientist, taking a strong stand on a subject as nebulous and unbelievable as the spirit world.

"I couldn't understand it," Dr. Crandon told me. "It did not fit into any pattern I had previously known about scientists. So I asked to meet him after his lectures. We talked for some time that first night. And we met again. We became friends. Sir Oliver suggested some reading for me, and I began, feeling somewhat foolish, but certainly intrigued."

Crandon found that many of the books on Sir Oliver's reading list had been written by well-known scientists. And the more he read the more he came to doubt his previous stand on immortality. He shed his atheism, became convinced of the survival of the soul, and shifted his active mind from Lincoln to psychic research.

At first Margery was amused by what she considered her husband's hobby. She had no interest in the subject; she had never experienced a psychic phenomenon, and her background was such that it could not intrigue her. She was satisfied in her Congregationalism, and her well-to-do family had never been concerned about such matters as the paranormal. Most of them had been motivated in much the same fashion as was her brother Walter, then dead, who had been a civil engineer.

But as Roy Crandon's "hobby" became more absorbing, and as he began to spend more and more time talking about it to Margery and their friends, Margery became bored and then impatient and irritated. "I decided to show him how foolish it was," she told me, "and I made an appointment with the minister of the First Spiritualistic Church in Boston. He was a medium and I telephoned him to ask for a sitting. He said to come the next morning.

"I knew perfectly well nothing would happen, for it was all silly, and the next morning, before my appointment at the church, I went riding with a friend. We didn't even bother to change from our riding clothes, and went in just the way we were."

They entered the minister's study, where he went into trance, and there the course of Margery's life was changed.

Within minutes two strange voices began to speak through the unconscious medium. Each said his name was Walter. One purported to be her dead uncle; the other asserted he was her dead brother, Walter Stinson.

Margery Crandon was amused but intrigued. This was indeed a magnificent trick, but how had the medium known about her uncle and her brother? She said, "One of you says you are my brother Walter. If this is so give me some evidence that will identify you." She turned to her companion and waited; she shifted her riding boots on the floor.

Walter said, "I hope you won't have the trouble with *those* riding boots that you had in Canada when you and I went riding." Then he correctly named the ponies they had ridden that day.

Margery was astounded. As she told me later, "His reference to trouble with my boots was absolutely weird, for he could be referring to only one thing. And the minister could not have known about it, any more than he could have known the names of the horses.

"Walter and I had been riding; we lived on a ranch in Canada then, and my horse got mired in a swamp. I had to dismount, and then like a fool I got stuck, too. I was wearing very tight riding boots and I couldn't even wriggle my foot out. So Walter dismounted and cut the boot off my leg with his pocketknife."

During the remainder of the sitting Walter told his sister that he was one of "a group of spirits in the other world which was interested in giving proof of survival to the living. But we want to do this along scientific lines; we're not much interested in bringing messages from the departed—that's old home stuff. But we are willing and eager to demonstrate our abilities with physical objects; we can do things that the living cannot do and which you cannot explain, and we would like to prove this."

Walter instructed his sister to form a circle of friends who would have patience and who would be in sympathy with the purpose of the experiments. He asked that this circle of friends sit in a darkened room around a table, with their hands on the table top, "keeping a closed circle by having contact with each other through fingers lightly touching."

Margery Crandon was more than slightly confused when she returned home to tell her husband what she had heard. Such an experience was completely alien to her, and it was far from what she had expected. Her husband suggested that they follow Walter's advice, and she agreed. For several nights the Crandons and several close friends sat silently in the dark touching fingers lightly and waiting for response. But there was consistent failure.

Then one night about a week after they had begun they heard faint taps on the table. Each night the taps grew stronger, and they became dependable—they were heard at each sitting.

The results were limited to these taps, now vigorous, for about a month, and then one night Margery suddenly went into trance and a voice, quite different from her own, began to speak faintly through her. It said it was Walter, her dead brother.

From that night on the Margery mediumship—and Walter—made such rapid progress that it was soon known around the world. Psychical research societies in many countries seized upon her remarkable abilities to pursue their studies, and 10 Lime Street was visited by hundreds of psychologists, scientists, and scholars. She was investigated by professional men from more than thirty countries, and gave sittings in England under the auspices of the British Society for Psychical Research.

I met Margery one summer in the early twenties when I was teaching in the graduate school of Boston University. While reading a Boston newspaper I noticed an article about a remarkable case of psychic mediumship which was taking place in the home of the eminent Boston surgeon Dr. L. R. G. Crandon. I telephoned Dr. Crandon and told him of my interest in psychic phenomena. I told him that I had studied under William James and that it had been James who had awakened my interest. I cannot say that Professor James's name acted as a password, but I do suspect it had some influence. At any rate Roy Crandon said, "I'll be delighted to meet another Harvard man. Let's set a date for you to come over."

Thus began twelve years of association with the famous and controversial mediumship of Margery—one of the most intriguing, fascinating, and mysterious events of my life.

To experience the events at 10 Lime Street was not only to get glimpses of wondrous, unexplainable things; it was to meet some of the outstandingly curious minds in the nation. At nearly every one of the many sittings I attended in the Crandon home I met outstanding scientists, psychologists, ministers, and professional men from all parts of the world. And frequently I took friends with me—men such as Julius Seelye Bixler, who taught with me in the department of religion at Smith and later became president of Colby College, and the late William Allen Neilson, president of Smith College. Both men showed an intelligent interest in the Margery phenomena, and Seelye Bixler had thoroughly studied William James and James's interest in mediums.

There was a routine to a sitting at Lime Street. After the evening's guests had assembled in the first-floor sitting room and introductions had been completed, we all climbed the stairs to the third-floor séance room. This was an austere, almost barnlike chamber about sixty feet long and fifty feet wide. In its center was a large, bare, rectangular oak table that could seat about twelve persons. At one end of the table stood Margery's cabinet, an especially constructed, fraudproof compartment that resembled a public telephone booth. Its upper half was glass-enclosed; it had a single door that locked; and at each side there were apertures through which Margery thrust her hands so that they could be securely tied from the outside.

The room had only one door, and after it was closed, and Margery was securely locked in the cabinet, visitors frequently piled books waist-high against it so that in the tense excitement of the dark séance no one could enter secretly.

Although most of the visitors to 10 Lime Street had immense faith in the integrity of both the Crandons, they were also intelligent people who were quite ingenious in guarding against any possible hoax or fraud. We had no reason to doubt the Crandons—they never received a single cent of payment for the thousands of sittings, and a mammoth, prolonged hoax by these two people was alien to their characters—but we were insistent upon eliminating every possible rational explanation for what we witnessed. For if we eliminated the possible and the phenomena still persisted, then perhaps, indeed, were we treading on the edge of new knowledge.

And the Crandons agreed that such precautions should be taken. They, too, were searching for answers and were eager to receive the evidence that Walter had promised and was producing. This is the reason why the cabinet had been built—designed by a frequent visitor who wanted to eliminate the possibility that Margery or her husband or a confederate were manipulating the phosphorescent rings or identifying the concealed objects we brought with us and revealed only in total darkness. This was the reason for the books piled against the door; this was the reason why, when Walter began to speak clearly and loudly from all parts of the room and whistle with such piercing clarity, Margery often filled her mouth with water or with marbles before she went into trance, and emptied her mouth when the sitting was completed.

Before each sitting a woman visitor, frequently a medical doctor, would strip Margery to the buff and examine her thoroughly to make sure that she was not concealing anything in any of the orifices of her body. Then Margery would be dressed only in slippers and a wraparound robe that had been searched. In the cabinet she sat on a plain wooden library chair with her ankles strapped to the chair legs, often with adhesive tape, sometimes with wire and lead seals. Her neck was held by a band of leather fastened to the back of the chair so that she could move her head only a few inches. At some sittings visitors sat next to her, outside the cabinet, holding her hands even though they were taped or wired or tied, so that there could be not the slightest possibility that she could, Houdinilike, wriggle from her bonds. And frequently Dr. Crandon was subject to similar control, with visitors holding his legs and arms to prevent any possibility that he could be responsible for the phenomena in that room.

Yet when the lights were out and we sat around the table in pitch blackness or in the faint glow of a dim red light we witnessed some of the most strange phenomena ever seen by humans.

When I first began to visit Lime Street the mediumship was in its early stages; Walter's voice was faint and his performance limited. The voice still came through Margery's vocal chords; it was not Margery's voice, but her body was being used as a mechanical device. As time went on the voice grew stronger and later began to speak from any part of the room. No longer was it dependent on Margery's throat; it became what is known as an independent voice.

I was present many times when Walter's voice was as clear as that of any person in the circle. And it was absolutely fascinating and startling to hear him wander about the room. At times his voice would be close to my ear, whispering some very personal comment about me or my family; at other times it would come from a far corner of the room, or from outside the room, beyond the door piled waist-high with books, or from the center of the table. It was utterly unlike any voice I have heard through ventriloquism; it was clear and sharp and distinct.

Once one of us asked Walter to explain his voice. "How can I talk to you?" he laughed. "Simple. I take ectoplasm from Margery while she is in trance. I make a voice box out of it and use it to create sound vibrations. Your own voice box does the same thing; so does a radio speaker. But while you use your own bodies to create your voices, or metal and paper and electricity in a radio, I use Margery's ectoplasm and my own vibrations."

Ectoplasm, we all knew, is filmy, plastic material which emerges at times from the mouth, nose, ears, or other orifices of a medium in trance and is able to take form and to exert physical pressure. I have seen it many times, sometimes as a solid substance and at other times as a vapor. Before the medium comes out of a trance the ectoplasm returns to the medium's body.

Walter frequently utilized the ectoplasm from Margery's body, and some of his demonstrations were astonishing. One night two professors from the faculty of the Massachusetts Institute of Technology arrived with their arms full of equipment. One carried a delicate chemist's scales in a glass-enclosed cabinet which was capable of being locked. The other carried two cameras, one with a conventional glass lens, the other with a quartz lens.

The chemist's scale was placed in the center of the table with its scalepans precisely balanced and its cabinet securely locked. Then we sat back, each professor ready with his camera and its flash equipment. Margery went into trance and Walter greeted us in his usual flippant, boisterous manner.

"Well," he said, "you want a new trick performed tonight."

One of the MIT scientists said, "What do you think you can do?"

And in the dim light of the small red bulb Walter said, "I'll make an ectoplasmic hand and I'll move your scalepans up and down while the cabinet is still locked. And you can take pictures with those two cameras you brought if you like."

Usually when Walter formed an ectoplasmic hand we would see a thin vapor emerge from Margery's nose and mouth. It would soon penetrate the glass wall of the cabinet and come to rest on the table top. Gradually it would become less ethereal, more solid, and then at its end would be formed a tiny, perfect human hand, even to fingernails. It was the size of a baby's hand. But tonight we saw nothing.

We waited and finally I asked, "Walter, can you tip one scalepan down until it touches the bottom of the cabinet?"

"Certainly," Walter's voice replied.

Now in the dim red light we could see the left scalepan begin to dip and its companion rise from the point of equilibrium. We could see nothing else, no weights, no ectoplasm, no possible source of physical energy. Two flash cameras exploded in the darkness as the visiting professors took their pictures.

"Walter," I asked, "do you mind if we attempt something else?"

"Not at all, Parson," he replied.

Then one of the professors unlocked the cabinet and I placed a penknife and a key ring on one scalepan. It plunged to the bottom of the cabinet and we relocked the case.

"Now Walter," I asked, "can you bring the scales to a level position?"

And the scales tipped to a perfectly level balance. Another visitor asked the weighted scales to go to the top and the empty pan to go to the bottom. The scales responded as requested.

When the sitting ended the two MIT men returned to their laboratories and developed the two plates they had exposed in the dimly lighted room. The film exposed through the ordinary glass lens showed us only what our eyes had seen: a chemist's scale without weights yet with the scale beam tipped askew. The other picture, taken with the quartz lens, revealed a tiny hand resting on the lower scalepan. Although we know that a quartz lens transmits ultra-violet light while an ordinary glass lens is opaque to it, this is only a tantalizing fragment of information; it advances us little toward an explanation. We could not see the ectoplasmic hand ourselves; the ordinary camera lens could not see it, but the quartz lens could.

On another evening when Walter had produced an ectoplasmic hand while Margery was in a deep trance, I asked him if he could follow my instructions in manipulating the hand.

"I'll try," he replied.

The ectoplasm, so far as I could observe, came from Margery's nose, terminating in a perfectly formed tiny hand on the table in front of me. I placed a handkerchief on the table and asked Walter to raise it and wave it. The hand immediately took firm hold of the handkerchief and waved it in the air. After it had been returned to the table I asked that the hand pull it off the table. This was also done, and I retrieved it from the floor and again placed it on the table. My third request was that the handkerchief be drawn across the full length of the long table. The hand took hold of the linen and swished it swiftly as I had requested.

Dr. Brewer Eddy then produced a twenty-five-cent piece and asked Walter to take it from his hand and place it in the hand of some other member of the circle. Immediately the tiny ectoplasmic fingers lifted the coin from Dr. Eddy's hand, and Walter's voice said, "Parson, hold out your palm." I did so and the quarter dropped into my fingers. "Now I'll take it back," Walter said and I felt the hand touch mine. It was cold and lifeless, but it moved and it exerted pressure.

Now science has always claimed that telekinesis, the movement of objects without normal physical force, does not exist in the scientific realm. Similarly some psychologists assert that there can be no survival of personality when the physical brain ceases to function. Yet I have seen telekinesis, at 10 Lime Street and at other places, and these facts defy orthodox science and psychology. And often as I attempt to equate the laws of physical science with the questions of psychical research I remember the words of Bishop George Berkeley, the great eighteenth-century Irish philosopher: "The only reality of this apparent world is what our senses bring us."

Walter's personality was indeed intriguing. Margery once told me that in life her brother Walter was a comparatively irreligious materialist, with an engineer's very practical turn of mind and a wry, flip sense of humor. In death he had changed little. He almost invariably addressed me as "the Parson," and my friend Dr. Brewer Eddy—a man filled with almost boundless nervous energy—he twitted by calling him "the flea," because he was restless and fidgeted in his chair. Walter seemed to take great joy in telling jokes concerning the people in the circle, and his laughter at our discomfiture was infectious. He was a most human and most humorous spirit.

He took obvious pride in his whistling ability, and there was some justification for his immodesty. Never have I heard such a remarkable whistler; he warbled, he had range, he had volume, and he had an almost unlimited repertoire. Often he whistled while he performed his acts of levitation and telekinesis, and sometimes his whistling was most disturbing. Once, after promising to demonstrate just how independent he was of physical matter, he whistled himself through the closed door and out into the hallway. We heard his whistling through the door and then it returned to the séance room. Apparently he could pass through an oak door and whistle from the other side as easily as I can pass through a bank of fog. Yet Margery herself could hardly whistle a note—many girls have been raised to believe that whistling is unladylike—and during many of Walter's whistling concerts Margery's mouth contained water or marbles or both.

Walter seemed proud that he could produce phenomena that could not be explained by any known natural causes. He seemed delighted that his accomplishments confounded some of the world's most alert scientists; his pride was that of a well-trained athlete successfully defending his title against a challenger in a well-fought contest; like that of a fine cabinetmaker who has added another superb piece of furniture to his inventory. Often he emphasized that his one main interest, similar to that of those "working with me on this side," was to give irrefutable evidence of survival in scientifically controlled experiments.

I have seen, not once but many times, a luminous ring of cardboard passed into Margery's cabinet by some member of the circle who unlocked the slot in the booth's door, and then watched the ring be seized immediately by a visible terminal of ectoplasm that waved it over Margery's head and swooped it in circles on the inside of the cabinet. And this happened while Margery was in trance, while her head was fastened to the chair with a leather collar, her ankles strapped to the chair legs, and her hands securely fastened and held by sitters outside the cabinet.

Walter scorned what he apparently considered amateur, unsophisticated, and unscientific evidence of survival—the delivering of messages from departed friends. Although he never used the phrase, he left us with the impression that he disliked being a messenger boy. I remember once when I asked him, "Walter, can you contact other spirits who have passed over?"

His reply was succinct and sarcastic, obviously referring to the telephone. "Can you talk with persons who live across the continent or in Europe?" And then he changed the subject and ignored any inferred request.

However, occasionally he would yield, although it was obvious that he considered such things as wasteful and distasteful. Once he consented to attempt to contact a very dear friend of mine. "I'll give it a try," he said brusquely, and then added, "Just tell me his name and where he died."

"His name," I said, "is the Reverend H. Roswell Bates. I was his assistant for three—"

"Never mind the history," Walter interrupted with some impatience. "Just tell me where he died."

"In Peru," I replied.

There was a piercing, warbling whistle and then silence in the séance room there on the third floor of a fine old house at the foot of Beacon Hill. And while I waited for Walter I thought of Roswell Bates. We had been like brothers. For three years while I was at Union Theological Seminary I had been his assistant at the Spring Street Presbyterian Church in New York City, where he had been minister. Before his marriage we had shared quarters in the Neighborhood House next to the church. If there was any man I had known well, and whom I missed very much, it was Roswell Bates.

In about ten minutes Walter spoke. "Your friend Bates is very good-looking." I could not deny this, for Roswell had been a handsome man.

"Bates can't talk to you himself," Walter said. "He doesn't have the power to communicate." And then in the short silence that followed I heard a faint whisper: "Hello, Ralph."

"Well," Walter said, "he *does* have some juice." There was silence for a while and then Walter said, "But I guess it's all gone. I'll relay for you, Parson. What do you want to know?"

I said, "If this is indeed my friend Roswell Bates, I want him to give me a message that will identify him to me."

The message electrified me. It was: "He says to tell Ralph that he has a dozen socks and ties and they all match." There could be no doubt about the identity of the person sending the message.

Often when we had lived together in Neighborhood House I teased Roswell about his socks and ties and his underdeveloped sense of color. He was just as likely to wear a blue tie with yellow socks as he was to mix purple and brown. Not that this was a tremendously important matter, but Roswell preached at many schools and colleges and at student conferences, and girls seem to notice such matters and be distracted by them. Often he asked me to help him select color combinations that would not clash, and my advice had been what was then common college practice: make ties and socks match, brown with brown, green with green, or shades thereof.

This little problem had become quite a joke with us, and once at a conference, I wrote a song about his dilemma. One verse was:

> Here's to Herbert Roswell Bates,
> His socks and ties are always mates;
> His panamas and flannels white
> Attract the students, day and night.

There was really only one person in the world who could have sent me this message now coming from Walter through Margery. If a stranger had stopped me on Broadway and handed me that communication I would have known instantly the identity of the sender—Roswell Bates. And at the Crandons' the possibility was *so* slim that Margery or Dr. Crandon or any other person there could ever have heard of Roswell Bates, let alone this tiny facet of his personality or the song I had written so many years before. It was information that only Roswell could have known.

That evening Walter relayed other information from Roswell: personal information about his family and about the work he was doing on the other side of death.

Some years later at another sitting Walter again reluctantly yielded to my request for "old home stuff" and brought me into contact with my sister Anna. That night we had been experimenting in total darkness with wooden letter blocks, Walter manipulating them to spell out words and messages. When he agreed to contact Anna we heard movement in the pile of blocks on the table and heard four of them drop at my feet.

Then Walter said, "Your sister Anna is here. Turn on the light." We did so and on the floor near my chair were four blocks, perfectly aligned, spelling "Anna." We thought Walter might end the contact with my sister there, but he continued, relaying Anna's words, and she talked with me for some minutes about her husband and four children.

I was fortunate to be present one night when Walter demonstrated one of his most unusual experiments. This was the production of his own thumbprint in dental wax, and over a period of years Walter produced more than a hundred prints. It started one night when one of the most persistent investigators of the Margery mediumship asked Walter if he could leave behind him some physical evidence of his identity. "Can you make fingerprints?" he asked.

"I don't know," Walter said, with some doubt in his voice. "But let's try."

Subsequently, using only dental wax, a cloth, and two pans of water—one boiling and one cold—fingerprints were produced with startling regularity, not only at 10 Lime Street but in private homes where the control of the experiments was even more stringent than at the Crandons', if such was possible. They were pressed into the hot-water-softened slabs of wax, and were both positive and negative; sometimes they were mirror prints.

The method was simple enough. The night I witnessed the phenomenon the Crandons were following the steps as outlined by Walter. Before the lights were turned out, a kettle of boiling water and an empty bucket were placed on the floor near the table. An empty pan, a pan filled with cold water, and a linen cloth were arranged on a table. Then, after Margery had gone into trance in complete darkness—even the red lights were extinguished during these experiments—a member of the séance group produced the slabs of dental wax that had been marked for identification and to prevent substitution. Boiling water was poured into the empty pan, and the linen cloth draped across the top so that it would fall to the bottom yet leave its ends out of the hot water.

Then one of the marked wax slabs was slid to the pans and Walter took over, whistling and talking while he worked. We could hear the splash as the wax dropped into the water and Walter continued to chatter while the heat softened it. After a few minutes we heard more splashing and Walter said, "Whew, the water's pretty hot tonight!" We knew he was removing the slab by lifting the dry ends of the cloth, because when the fingerprint experiments had first begun he had complained that the hot water was harming the ectoplasmic hand, and had suggested some other method of removing the wax slab from the pan.

I heard movement on the table, as he made his thumbprint in the soft wax, and then a splashing sound as he slid the slab into the cold water to set the imprint. He said, "All right, turn on the lights. I think we have a good print tonight." And we did—a perfect imprint of a human thumb.

Extended investigation by the research officer of the American Society for Psychical Research established evidence that this print and almost all of the others produced by the Margery mediumship were identical with the lifetime right thumbprint of Walter Stinson, Margery's brother. A few of the prints could not be identified, and some of them, Walter said, were the impressions of colleague spirits who aided him in the experiments at 10 Lime Street.

Perhaps even more remarkable than Walter's ability to produce fingerprints was his facility at what is called cross correspondence by researchers in psychic phenomena. In this spectacular phenomenon, an experience repeated in many parts of the world through many different psychic mediums, a so-called "spirit" communicates simultaneously with several mediums separated by long distances, sometimes hundreds of miles. He chops his message into as many parts as there are receivers or mediums, and sends one part to each of them. When the portions are joined they make the complete message. In essence this is thought transference, but instead of being between humans it is between a spirit and several humans.

The particular case of cross correspondence that I witnessed involved three groups—those of us with Margery in Boston; a group 400 miles away in Niagara Falls, New York, with the medium Dr. Henry Hardwicke; and a group 175 miles away in New York City with George Valentine, a man of remarkable psychic power. With each group sat members of the American Society for Psychical Research.

Walter's task this night was to transmit a portion of his message to Margery and have her record it while in trance, and to send the other portions to Dr. Hardwicke in Niagara Falls and to George Valentine in New York City, both of whom would also be in trance.

We saw Margery go into trance about 9:30, and Walter chatted with us for a few minutes, greeting those who were in the circle and commenting, "Well, I'm going to have to move like lightning tonight. I've got to watch over you people here even while I go to Niagara Falls and New York. Now here's what I'm going to do. I'll give Margery an arithmetic problem and part of a sentence. The answer to the problem and the words necessary for the completion of the sentence will be deposited in New York and Niagara Falls. You have your arrangements made for getting the other parts back here to you?"

We nodded in the séance room, and almost immediately—at 9:50 P.M., according to the official transcript of the sitting—Margery picked up a pencil and wrote, "11 x 2." Beneath it she wrote, "kick a dead;" then stopped writing. That was all, and Walter was no longer with us at 10 Lime Street. All members of the group signed this sheet to validate the experiment, and Dr. Crandon telephoned the Valentine group in New York City.

There Dr. T. H. Pearson, then chairman of the research committee of the American Society for Psychical Research, reported that at exactly 9:50 Valentine had written, "equals 2," and "No one ever stops to." The message was signed, "Walter."

Not much later a telegram from the Hardwicke group in Niagara Falls reported to us. At precisely 9:50 Dr. Hardwicke had gone into trance. With his right hand still in contact with the left hand of his neighbor, he picked up a pencil and wrote rapidly and accurately on two sheets of paper in the center of the table. One sheet read, "2." On the other was the word "horse."

We assembled the three parts. It was not difficult, for not a word was missing or confused. The arithmetical problem read, "11 x 2 equals 22." The sentence, which Margery later told us was one of Walter's favorite sayings when he was alive, was, "No one ever stops to kick a dead horse."

Walter—or Margery mediumship, or both— was indeed remarkable. In twenty-seven consecutive sittings, some of which I witnessed, Walter made more than two hundred correct identifications of playing cards selected at random in the dark from a newly opened deck brought to the sittings with the manufacturer's seal still intact. Not once was he in error, and the mathematical possibilities of such a performance are astronomical. Through Walter, Margery developed the facility of automatic writing while in trance, and the scrap book which contained the results included messages in ancient Norwegian, which were identified later by a visiting Norwegian scholar, and portions of the Chinese classics written in Chinese ideographs and later verified and translated by two Chinese scholars at Harvard.

Especially because I am a minister my experiences at 10 Lime Street have given me much to ponder. Often I ask myself, "But what spiritual significance is there in all this?" Not long ago a friend wrote me that she was disappointed in her study of psychic phenomena because "the persons who claim to communicate do not seem to have reached a much higher spiritual level than when they were on earth." Apparently she expected a sudden and miraculous change, a transformation from prejudice and selfishness into generous and spiritual idealism.

I find nothing in the teachings of Jesus to substantiate her desire. The Scripture says, "Whatsoever a man sows that shall he also reap." Selfish people remain selfish; prejudiced minds remain closed to liberal thought; but unselfish spirits and those who "hunger and thirst after righteousness, shall be filled." It may take a long time and many experiences to transform an evil spirit into holiness. Those that love darkness will hardly rejoice suddenly in the light.

As a minister I am concerned not only with evidence of survival but also with the *quality* of that survival in terms of the *values* retained or gained. What does seem significant to me in this study of the paranormal is that evidence of survival and of continued personality is being discovered: proofs that memory, affections, and relationships survive the death of the physical body. This is what religious faith has maintained through the centuries—that man is built on the scale of two worlds, one transient and fleeting, the other eternal and immortal.

Without survival of personality, Christian immortality, with its emphasis on the importance of the individual's awareness of values and relationships, is impossible. If after death we are simply absorbed into an unconscious existence—the Hindu's concept of immortality—or merely remembered in the minds of loved ones left behind, or "immortalized" in deeds done in the flesh, there is no immortality. Not the immortality of which Christ spoke and St. Paul bore witness to; not the faith which has been nurtured and sustained through the centuries.

What are the things that are implicit in the gospel we preach and which we dare to believe is true? They are the value of the individual in the sight of a living God, the evolution of the spirit in sonship with that God, the infinite possibilities for greater and more significant service in an afterlife, for so many of us are denied that opportunity in this fleeting earthly life. And we do dare to believe, acting on faith where we have no proof, and here is where the intellect acts heroically.

Such equating the psychical with the spiritual does not help us much with an analysis of Walter, nor answer our questions about the "higher spiritual level" of those who purport to live in another world. But perhaps I have given an incomplete picture of Walter simply because his ability as a performer was so spectacular. Although he was indifferent to religion in life, and even after death, and treated ministers at his sittings with irreverent humor, he did often make significant—although unorthodox—expressions of religious faith.

And once he sent a religious poem through Margery. He had written it, he said, because he had been informed of a conference of ministers and religious leaders to be held at the Isle of Shoals in New Hampshire. Margery sent me a copy of it, and it reads:

> The noblest work on earth, within my ken
> Is ministering to the souls of men.
> And if our vision's true and God is near,
> His voice will speak to you and you will hear,
> "Go ye out to all the world and preach for me
> The Gospel of Immortality."
> For God's in every man and man's divine
> For He hath said, "Let thy light so shine,"
> That unto all others a beacon it shall be,
> Helping and guiding on toward Immortality.
> Thou canst not help or guide the least one on
> If thou art not sure thyself the way is true;
> That is the reason I have come to you
> To make it simpler, clearer, unto thee,
> To find the way to Immortality.
> If thou hast helped just one poor, lonely soul
> To heal a wound and make it whole,
> Then hast thou seen God, and God shall dwell with thee,
> Making thee sure of Immortality.

When this poem—truly ghostwritten, to use the vernacular of our times—was transmitted, Walter asked that it be read at the religious conference. And his request was granted by a Unitarian minister who had been present at 10 Lime Street when the poem was received.

6

A Bridge from this World to the Next

One evening my first cousin Dr. Roland G. Usher, reading the evening paper in St. Louis, Missouri, reached the end of his academic restraint. He went to the telephone and called a friend, one of the editors of the newspaper.

"Who," he asked his friend, "who in the world is Patience Worth?"

"She writes poems for us," the editor laughed. "We publish them."

"I know," Roland said. "I read them. I read them every month or so, every time you publish them. Did you know they're Elizabethan English? Perfect Elizabethan English?"

"Well, I didn't know they were perfect but I thought they were pretty good. You're the Elizabethan expert. What's the trouble?"

"There's no trouble," Roland said. "I'm just bursting with curiosity. Almost every one of these poems has a word or a phrase that is unfamiliar to me, and then I think, 'Ah, I've caught her.' And I go to my Elizabethan dictionary and there it is—the word does exist and it's used correctly, too. Now who is Patience Worth?"

"She's a housewife here in St. Louis. An ordinary woman with an eighth-grade education. Her name's Curran. Pearl Lenore Curran. About thirty-five. She's the wife of John Curran, the state immigration commissioner. What else do you want to know?"

Roland laughed. "Where did she learn Elizabethan English? And where did she learn to write poetry?"

"She didn't," the editor said. "The stuff comes over Mrs. Curran's Ouija board. Patience Worth is a ghost."

"Oh, come on," Roland said. "I really want to know."

"And I'm really telling you," the editor said. "I've checked it out myself. If you want to meet Mrs. Curran I think I can arrange it."

And so Roland met Mrs. Curran, witnessed the Ouija-board writing of Patience Worth; and through Roland, some time later, so did I.

Pearl Curran's meeting with Patience Worth was as unlikely as finding a beatnik minister in a Baptist church. It began on a July evening of 1913 during the nation-wide Ouija-board fad that occupied the American recreational mind in much the same fashion as have mah-jongg and canasta. Mrs. Curran and a friend, Mrs. Emily Hutchings, sat toying with a new Ouija board while they waited for their husbands to return from a meeting. They had played with the board before with no results, but this night the pointer seemed to be activated suddenly, moving rapidly from one letter to another, spelling out the sentence: "Many moons ago I lived. Again I come. Patience Worth my name."

"It was very strange," Mrs. Curran told me later when I first called on her. "We were not frightened, for we knew that a Ouija board was supposed to bring messages. But I thought Emily was pushing the pointer, and she thought I was doing it. And to carry on the joke I asked aloud, 'When did you live?' The pointer moved to four numbers: 1649, and then spelled out the sentences, 'I come from England across the sea. Let me hold your ear for a lesson I would teach.' "

Patience never did clarify, in the fifteen years of her communication with Mrs. Curran, whether 1649 was the date of her birth or of her arrival in America. But a summary of her messages indicates that she was a small, redheaded English girl from Dorsetshire who emigrated to the Massachusetts Colony, lived on Cape Cod, and was killed during an Indian massacre during King Philip's war in either 1675 or 1676. Apparently she died a spinster, rather unusual during the women-sparse days of the early colonies.

As a spirit she was as unlike Margery's Walter as is an owl to a meadowlark, although both had quick tongues and sharp wits, with Patience being perhaps more acid. While Walter concentrated on physical phenomena—levitation, fingerprints, scale-balancing—which he insisted be done in darkness while Margery was in trance, Patience wanted merely to write poetry and novels. And she wrote hundreds of poems and three long novels on the Currans' Ouija board, doing so in broad daylight or bright lights while Mrs. Curran was completely conscious, and without what some critics call "the hocus-pocus of the séance room."

Mrs. Curran once told me, "The only sensation I have when Patience is sending messages through the Ouija board is a slight sense of someone touching me lightly on the top of the head, and sometimes I seem to see the scenes that Patience is describing."

In her writings Patience described seashore cliffs, a monastery, and a village connected with her childhood. She frequently referred to the sea, although Mrs. Curran had never been near the ocean, having lived her life in the Midwest. Patience spoke of birds, flowers, and trees that are native only to England, had an intimate knowledge of archaic forms of the English language, and often wrote of customs long since abandoned in England but common during the golden age of the Elizabethan period when Shakespeare and Spenser were writing their great works.

A skeptical newspaperman, Casper S. Yost, attempted to expose Mrs. Curran as a fraud, but became convinced of the reality of Patience after he had traveled to England and successfully identified many of the places she had described. In many respects the case of Patience Worth was a preview of the case of Bridey Murphy except that there was no hint of reincarnation with Patience.

As the relationship between Mrs. Curran and Patience developed, the messages came more rapidly from the Ouija board, and later Mrs. Curran discarded it because she found she could do automatic writing—writing directly on a sheet of paper as if she were a secretary recording dictation from a silent, unseen employer. Actually Mrs. Curran never acquired any equanimity about her ability; it confused her because she could not explain it, and she was afraid of being considered queer by her friends and neighbors. Her greatest interest was singing, and she had a horror of being considered a medium—which of course she was, whether she liked it or not.

My first visit to Mrs. Curran took place in 1917, shortly after I had returned from teaching in Turkey and was on a speaking trip to American colleges. I stopped off to see cousin Roland in St. Louis, where he was head of the history department of Washington University, and we went with another professor to call on Mrs. Curran, whom Roland by then had visited many times.

"I can't explain it, Ralph," he said on the way to the Curran home. "Unless, of course, it is just what it purports to be. Mrs. Curran is nice enough, and really a very solid woman, but she's not a great booklover and never has been; she's not interested in things intellectual. It's simply not credible that she could have acquired such detailed knowledge of either English history or the language of that period. In addition she's simply not capable of writing such good poetry or such good novels."

I nodded, agreeing with Roland, for I knew the background for his judgment. He had three degrees in English history and had specialized in the Elizabethan period, studying at Harvard, in Paris, and at Oxford and Cambridge. He certainly could be considered an expert witness.

When we arrived at the Curran home I saw nothing exceptional about the household or about Mrs. Curran. She was a tall thin woman, rather pleasant and gentle and not very talkative. I sensed that she was somewhat shy. Her house was typically middle class, with an upright piano and stacks of sheet music in the living room. There were a few magazines and a very small shelf of light, popular novels, but these seemed to be the limit of the Currans' interest in literature of any kind.

We chatted for a few minutes about the first visit of Patience Worth to the Curran home, and then Mrs. Curran asked me if I would like to sit with her at the Ouija board. She sat with her fingers lightly touching the pointer and closed her eyes. I placed my fingers near hers and we waited. Roland Usher sat on my left; the other professor sat on my right, pad and pencil ready.

Soon, in the silence of the well-lighted room, the planchette began to move slowly. As it stopped at a letter Roland read it aloud and the professor recorded it. Then the pointer picked up speed, at times going so rapidly that our recorder could not keep up and would ask to have letters repeated. The first messages were simple greetings to Mrs. Curran and to us.

Then, aloud, I asked, "Patience, can you give me some message about Turkey? I have just returned from there."

Now the planchette began to move with such rapidity that I could not follow the sense of the message. Roland intoned the letters each time the pointer paused for a short moment, and his colleague began to fill page after page with letters, unspaced and unpunctuated. Mrs. Curran sat with her eyes closed but certainly not in trance, for during the rare and slight pauses she opened them and spoke to us in a normal voice.

Finally after twenty or thirty minutes the planchette ceased moving and we turned to the message. When we had broken the letters into words and the words into sentences we had a beautiful poem, in free verse, titled "The Land of the Pashas."

It told of camel bells, of the perfume of the bazaars, of the minarets of the mosques, and of other authentic characteristics of Turkey. Then, remembering my tour of the colleges, I asked Patience if she would give me something inspirational that might be useful in my talks. Immediately the planchette went into action, and an even more beautiful poem, "Inspiration," came over the board.

To my great regret I sent these poems to a friend who was making a study of psychic phenomena, and foolishly—perhaps because I did not then recognize the significance of the experience—I did not make copies. These have been lost, but hundreds of her verses have been preserved and published. For example, the following, in which is found her faith:

If Thou shouldst demand, O Great God,
Why I love thee, how might I answer?
I might say, "This morning I saw wheat tickling the sunshine;
Yea, I saw a lark marking the heavens,
Grotesquely playing a jest with his song."
I might say that I saw a star shoot,
Leaving a little radiance streaking,
As though in an endeavor to write me a little whimsey message.
I might say, yea, I might say that I love Thee—
What for, O Gracious God, what for?
For Thy strength?
Kennin' well that Thou mightest take twixt Thy finger
And thumb the universe and send it streaking
As ashy dust across the ether,
Knocking the mountains one upon the other,
Making echoes like thunder.
For this? Nay, methinks I'd rather
Say I love Thee for the little swishing tassels
Whipping at the waters fitfully.
I like to think of this—
That Thou art then a youth, playing so.

Her verses on death and immortality can comfort all who are bereaved and those of us who are filled with doubts about the ultimate meaning of life and death. Her interpretation of the heart of Jesus' teaching is summed up in this short verse, which she wrote for a minister:

To deal justice; to make thy heart quick with mercy
And with understanding;
To make thy hand slow in dealing aught save mercy;
To make thee companionable fully with the day
In a sure understanding;
To measure thyself first, and find how light the measure is,
And lay that 'pon the beam of thy brother,
Ere thou measure him.

As a minister I find Patience revealing a spiritual quality far beyond that of the average church member. In hundreds of her verses, in the numerous proverbs she quoted to Mrs. Curran, in her many comments on life and its meaning, we discover in Patience Worth a wisdom and a spiritual insight such as we associate with prophetic spirits of all ages and of all people. And she has beautiful clarity in expressing herself. For example:

> There is nothing in all the preachments
> Of man, which either stimulates
> Or confounds me. I have known
> Since my soul first beheld that great,
> Stately beyond of which I was a part—
> I have known, I say, that God is.

But while I feel myself qualified to comment about Patience's spiritual attitudes, I know that I do not qualify as a literary critic. Fortunately, in regard to her literary output, I need not depend solely on my own judgment. The critics of the time seemed almost to fall over themselves in their praise of her work.

Braithwaite's Anthology of Magazine Verse for 1918, a collection of the year's best, included poems by Sara Teasdale, three by Amy Lowell, three by Vachel Lindsay, one by Edgar Lee Masters—and five by Patience Worth. The anthologists, of course, did not know that these verses were literally ghostwritten.

That year Patience Worth was named as one of "the outstanding authors of the year" and invited to a reception at the National Arts Club at which Amy Lowell and Rupert Hughes were two of the speakers. She declined the invitation with regrets. Later the Joint Committee of Literary Arts of New York recognized her as an outstanding novelist.

Her longest poem is "Tekla," a sixty-thousand-word dramatic story of peasant life in medieval England. Of it Dr. Franklin Prince, the executive research officer of the Boston Society of Psychical Research and a man who devoted years to a study of Patience and Mrs. Curran, wrote: "And let us not forget. . .that it was dictated in a total of about thirty-five hours only, intermingled with talk and a variety of miscellaneous literary material in the presence of witness, and through the mouth of a woman who up to that time had read little poetry, who had never practiced or studied the art of dramatic or poetical construction, and who through her days, during the period of dictation, was engaged in her household duties, singing at the piano, making and receiving calls, going to picture shows, and doing all the things which make up the life of an ordinary American woman of moderate circumstances."

Her first novel, *The Sorry Tale*, concerned the life of Christ in the Palestine of two thousand years ago. When it was published the book reviewer for the New York *Times* was enthusiastic, praising a "young and brilliant author who has produced a novel of unusual quality." Not knowing that the author was connected to the unseen end of a Ouija board, he praised her for her exhaustive study of the history of that period and assumed that she had traveled extensively in the Holy Land. Speaking of the novel's authenticity and credibility and of the Romans, Greeks, and Jews that people it, he wrote, ". . .as Kipling makes one smell and see India, just so in *The Sorry Tale* one is transplanted back to the Palestine of Jesus' day."

Another critic wrote, "It is the most remarkable piece of literature I have ever read. I have no hesitation in saying that this production is a world literary marvel."

By the time her second novel, *Hope Trueblood*, was published the world knew the real identity of Patience Worth, but such knowledge did not seem to disturb the critics; they judged the novel on its literary merits alone. The reviewer for the New York *Herald* wrote: "Whether in the body or in the spirit, the author of *Hope Trueblood* is singularly gifted with imagination, invention and the power of expression. The psychological analysis and dramatic power displayed in the narrative are extraordinary and stamp it as a work approximating absolute genius."

When it was published in England an English reviewer, obviously unaware that Patience *already* was immortal, wrote of the author: "A new writer who will take her seat among the immortals. This is a book over which generations of men and women will laugh and weep in days to come. . .a landmark of fiction."

The passage of years has not been kind to the gush raves of the critics, for the novels of Patience Worth have not stood up to the test of time; her "absolute genius" is forgotten, and no "generations of men and women" are laughing and weeping over her characters. While the novels of her contemporaries, Willa Cather and Dorothy Canfield Fisher and Sherwood Anderson, remain a part of American literature, Patience Worth's literary accomplishments were as impermanent as her spirit.

Perhaps *The Sorry Tale* is not "a world literary marvel," except in terms of its source, but Patience once told Mrs. Curran that one of her great "earth urges" had been to write a story about Christ, and certainly in *The Sorry Tale* she achieved her purpose.

And in *Hope Trueblood* she reveals a remarkable Christ-like insight into human needs and frailties; she strips bare all the petty prejudices in the minds of little men and illuminates their potential spiritual greatness.

In 1928 Patience told Mrs. Curran that her earthly work had been accomplished and that she was leaving. She asked Mrs. Curran to grant her a final request.

In a certain hospital in St. Louis, Patience said, a baby girl had just been born to a mother who already had more children than she could afford to feed, clothe, or educate properly. She named the specific ward and identified the bed by number.

"Please," Patience asked, "please visit the mother and offer to adopt the child. She will agree. Name the child Patience Worth."

Mrs. Curran adopted the tiny baby, named her Patience Worth Curran, and raised her into adulthood. That was the last ever heard of Patience Worth.

No one who has ever sat at a Ouija board with Mrs. Curran or has studied the mysterious case of Patience Worth can possibly avoid the question: "Who was Patience?" After his long study of the phenomena Dr. Franklin Prince writes, "Either our concept of what we call the subconscious must be radically altered, so as to include potentialities of which we hitherto have had no knowledge, or else some cause operating through, but not originating in, the subconsciousness of Mrs. Curran must be acknowledged."

Whatever conclusions we may reach, no one can read the poetry, the novels, the aphorisms of Patience Worth without being deeply affected. Her comments on religion and immortality and the inspiration and faith that flow from her can make us better, braver persons—if we can meet her challenge to live by a larger faith.

In a nuclear age when repressed fear is constantly with us and when confusion limits our horizons, the messages of Patience Worth can awaken in our minds and in our souls deeper conviction that the purposes of a good and loving God are ultimately beyond defeat.

As her words echo in our souls we can gain a triumphant faith in immortality and a testament that man is created on the scale of two worlds, not one. Patience is, for me, a bridge that helps us travel from this world to the next.

7

A Latent Power
in Us All

We all remember the parlor riddle that goes: If a coconut was dropped from a palm tree onto a rock on an uninhabited desert island in the middle of the Pacific Ocean, and there were no living things within a thousand miles, would that smashing coconut make a sound?

I cannot hazard how many generations of college students have delighted themselves with it, shifting sides as easily as a chameleon changes colors; worrying it as a puppy snarls and chews at a stolen slipper; in reality hoping that there is no answer, for then they will have to find something else to worry about.

One view about the coconut maintains that because there are no ears to hear the sound there is no sound; that sound exists only where it can be heard. The other view insists that of course sound is there; its parishioners say that vibrations—not ears—make sound, and that it exists even if it can't be heard; that to deny it is like insisting that because we do not happen to have a radio receiving set there are no radio waves in the ether.

The problem, of course, is one of definition, and to insist on definition at the beginning of this game is to remove its delight. But psychic research is not a game, and we cannot pervert the rules to maintain our amusement. We are shortsighted, indeed—and are certainly shortchanging our own intellects—if we maintain that psychic phenomena are nonexistent because we do not experience them. Actually there is an excellent, and exciting, possibility that an honest, patient, well-ordered study of the psychic can lead us to a scientifically sound solution to the enigma of death—a mystery which our forefathers solved by cramming it into the domain of pure faith. But we must be alert.

Long study in this field leads me to believe that all of us have at least some small degree of psychic power. In some of us this is refined to the point where we get such mediumships as Margery and Pearl Curran; in most of us the power is latent, waiting for an opportunity to emerge. And I have observed that a person's spirituality, his awareness and belief in God, has little connection with his ability to experience psychic phenomena. Atheists and agnostics, as well as persons who are indifferent about their professed religious attitudes, have demonstrated remarkable psychic power; and I have known persons with great spiritual vision and faith who have never experienced anything psychic.

Yet all around us are those who *are* in contact with the mysterious world of eternity. Although most Americans are somewhat reluctant about revealing their experiences, fearing they will be considered unusual or queer, there is hardly a group of ten or more persons assembled on the American mainland which does not contain someone who has brushed against the psychic. I am convinced that the paranormal is not the exclusive realm of a few gifted sensitives.

One of my Smith students, for example, shared a rare and wondrous experience that is unexplainable in terms of normal accepted knowledge but which is of a type sometimes recorded in the literature of psychic research.

One spring day during a school vacation my student—let's call her Jane—picked up a classmate for a drive from Taunton, Massachusetts, to New Haven, Connecticut. They drove in Jane's father's four-door sedan, chattering in the way of college girls and enjoying the golden bloom of the forsythia in the New England dooryards.

After about thirty minutes of driving, and while traveling a stretch of comparatively deserted road, they saw a little old lady standing at the roadside ahead of them. The woman waved at them as they approached, and smiled as they passed her.

Then Jane said to her companion, "I wonder if she wanted a ride?"
Her classmate laughed. "A hitchhiker at her age? Hardly."
But Jane slowed and looked in her rear-view mirror. The little lady was still standing there, watching the receding automobile. "Well, let's see if she does want a ride." And she backed down the road to the waiting woman.

She was a friendly old lady, about the age of Jane's grandmother, and she said she was on her way to visit her son in New Haven. She got into the back seat of the car, and although the woman did not say so, Jane assumed she had been waiting at the roadside for a bus, although obviously she must have walked some distance from her home to that particular isolated spot on the road.

As they rode along Jane said, in the blithe way of the young, "Oh, your son lives in New Haven? What's his name? I know people in New Haven."

And the little old lady told the girls her son's name and address, then seemed to settle back in quiet enjoyment of the ride.

After they had driven for about ten more minutes Jane's companion turned around to the back seat to talk to their passenger, and the little lady had vanished.

"Impossible," Jane gasped when they had stopped the car. "We didn't stop—or even slow down—since we picked her up. Do you think she fell out?"

They turned the car around and drove back to the spot where they had first seen the woman, but saw nothing.

"There's something wrong," Jane said. "She could be hurt. Let's go see her son." And remembering the address the woman had told them, they drove to New Haven and knocked on the door of the son's home.

Disturbed and bewildered, Jane blurted to the man who answered the door, "Are you expecting a visit from your mother?"

The man half smiled at her abruptness, shook his head and said, "No. Hardly. Mother died two months ago."

Now the girls, embarrassed and confused, started to leave the porch when Jane's companion turned and asked the man, "What does your mother—what did you mother—look like?"

His description was identical with that of the woman who had been riding with the girls, and he brought out a photograph of his mother which startled them. They left then without telling the man that they had seen her, for they knew he would not believe.

There are more of these experiences than we know, because participants are understandably reluctant to talk about them. Who wants to have his friends and neighbors shy away from him? But my frequent public talks about psychic phenomena have helped unearth many psychic experiences that otherwise would have remained concealed. My files are filled with letters, such as the following from a middle-aged mother who lives not far from my home in Massachusetts:

> I have been interested for a long time in the field of psychic phenomena, and I have read with interest a report of your own studies and experiences in this field. I am glad that someone in our neighborhood is interested in such phenomena from the student's angle.

A friend of mine and I have had some very interesting experiences in the way of messages that have come to us from those who have gone on ahead. This has been going on for over two years now. It has apparently risen spontaneously and there is no money involved. [Here the writer of the letter is explaining that she and her friend neither go to mediums who charge for their services nor charge others; thus money is eliminated as a motive for fraud.] Neither of us is a student of any such phenomena. It is all very new to us and we can understand it only through our own experience.

Those who give us messages sometimes tell their names; sometimes not. To me it appears bona fide, partly because the speed of the messages and their content seem to preclude any outside interference. The messages have been on many subjects, some profound, some counseling, some simply and purely humorous. Our messages have come from some we knew, and from others we have never met, but know by reputation. Some of those who came to us were members of our own families. Names were often given with evidential facts.

In a larger sense we are ordinary people. We are both married and have children, although my friend is a widow. We are not unusual by ourselves; only in this gift that has come to us. After the messages come, my friend seems exhausted. She, more than I, is psychic, although we both seem to have this gift. But she hears voices and does automatic writing in the handwriting of the sender and in his style of writing. We get very interesting and accurate historical facts and intelligent answers to many problems.

I wish we knew more about this field. I do not understand why this has come to us. We wish we knew what is the best use to make of this gift. I do know that it has changed our outlook on life, on death, on immortality, and on some problems of religion.

I have a very strong suspicion that many of our views on religion would change radically, as they have with these women, as a result of psychic contact. And I am sure that a lot of living Christians are going to be surprised Christians when they finally reach that spot they want to call heaven and discover that it really isn't as they have been told, have been taught, and have believed it to be.

I remember contacting, while teaching in Greece and doing some paranormal investigation with the Greek Society of Psychical Research, a Greek theologian who claimed to have lived and died in the Middle Ages. At the time I joined the Greek investigators they had been in contact with the spirit of the medieval priest for some months. He had told them he was rewriting, verse by verse, the Gospel according to St. Matthew, the first book of the New Testament, and giving the true meaning of the original.

During the hour-long sittings the investigators, speaking Greek with the priest, heard his revision of St. Matthew and questioned him about the exact meaning of every word written by St. Matthew. My own Greek was too limited to follow all the conversation, but it was translated to me by a friend sitting at my side.

The translation was quite interesting and exciting, for this spirit, who purported to be a former member of the Greek Orthodox Church, was giving us a most liberal interpretation of the Gospel passages. He seemed quite distressed that Jesus is so misunderstood by the church in Greece today. "Instead of following His teachings, especially in social and international problems," he said, "you are merely worshipping Him and the saints. This is not enough. This is not the total responsibilitiy of a Christian."

He said that he hoped his words, brought to the world through the Greek Society of Psychical Research, might open blind eyes to the truth. I do not know what ever happened to this new version of St. Matthew, but I am sure that it could not find favor among strictly orthodox leaders of the Greek Orthodox Chruch. As I remember this experience I think with some dismay of Hegel's cynical sentence: "The institution which is established to preserve the idea strangles it." Or, as Harnack says, "Constantine inoculated the world with Christianity and it escaped the disease."

Some of my other psychic experiences in Greece were not so philosophical but they were more dramatic in their physical manifestations. On the music faculty of the college was a young widow, an American Fulbright scholar, who had previously experienced contact with her dead husband, Tom. With another psychically sensitive young woman, an American-educated Greek girl who was also on the faculty, we formed a circle of four. Every two weeks throughout the winter we met for an evening of experimental table-tipping, sitting together with our joined fingers lightly touching the table top and hoping for the taps that would signify a paranormal contact.

Almost immediately we began to get messages from the widow's dead husband, Tom, and later from other intelligences. But Tom was more persistent, visiting us more frequently, and—perhaps because of his wife's presence—friendlier and more comfortable.

As we came to know him better I began to urge him to give us some physical manifestation, other than the tappings, of his presence. In other circles over the years I have made similar requests, have received promises, but no more than these. Tom, however, produced.

One night as we sat in our small basement dining room around the table I said, "Tom, can you open the door of this room?" His rapped answer was "Yes."

And as we waited on that breezeless night, each in plain sight of the others and with our fingers touching, the latched door unlatched itself and, squeaking, swung open.

Not many nights later Tom said that he would give us further physical demonstrations of his presence and his power. He would light the wall behind his wife, he said. With some sort of inaneness I asked, "Will it take long?" And Tom was polite about answering such a really meaningless question. "About five minutes," he replied.

And as we waited I mentally checked the possibilities of our fooling ourselves with natural sources, if perchance Tom failed. It was night, and our cottage was in a small village without street lights and situated where such a rare occurrence as a passing automobile could not shine its headlights in the window. I knew that not only was a lantern or a flashlight unlikely, but that I could recognize either; and as it turned out, the light that Tom did produce was as unlike a beam from a conventional source as are a barn swallow and a jet aircraft.

The light was not a subtle growth upon the wall; it was a sudden splash of illumination, bright and almost blinding, laid across the wall from floor to ceiling, from end to end, as if the stones behind the plaster were in reality continuous lighting panels such as are now used in some industrial construction. It made a thrilling moment for us. The brilliance lasted for about one minute and then vanished as swiftly as it had come, as if an electrical switch had been thrown.

Then in the silence of our wonder Tom rapped a question, almost childish with his delight at astounding us. "How did you like my light?" he asked. Our spontaneous gasps and our unconscious noddings answered him, and modestly he said that he was pleased.

Some time earlier, during the ten years I was chaplain at International College in Smyrna, Turkey, we witnessed a remarkable example of what is called post cognition, a paranormal experience during which a person sees events that took place in the past, or events that are then taking place at a distant point. The wife of one of the faculty members had this power. The most startling of her experiences transpired in 1922 during the Greek invasion of Turkey. Months previously the Greek expeditionary force had marched through the port of Smyrna and was then approaching Ankara, the capital of Turkey, almost four hundred miles inland.

One afternoon this psychic woman reported that she had seen a vision of a great battle being fought on the banks of a swift river. She saw men killing and being killed, watched the deployment of the troops, heard the shriek of overhead artillery and its explosive bursts as it detonated on the battlefield. She saw the battle in detail and told us she thought it was decisive.

A few days later we began to get reports of the battle of the Sakarya River, three hundred miles from Smyrna, where Mustafa Kemal defeated the invading Greeks in an engagement that broke the back of the invasion and drove the Greeks back into the Mediterranean Sea. Our friend's vision had occurred while this critical battle was in progress.

Some years later, when we had returned to the United States, I had the opportunity to meet a family that was unusual not only in its education and open-mindedness, but in the precise records it kept about its psychic experiences.

Like so many other initiations to paranormal ventures, this one began with a Ouija board brought home for family amusement. When the family's two daughters placed their fingers on the pointer, the response was immediate. The first completely coherent message was: "Do not take this too seriously. It is just as I used to come over for a plate of pea soup and a game of five hundred. Don't get too nervous; just relax and enjoy a chat. At times your current will be stronger; do you want me to come again?" It was signed "T. L.," the initials of an internationally famous engineer who had been a close friend of the family's.

From the beginning, the family members made comprehensive notes on each experiment, signing them and collecting them in a large notebook. The records include not only the questions and answers of each session but also the comments of the experimenters about the sessions.

For example, one note, written after one of the daughters had developed the ability of automatic writing, reads: "We are certain that the control was absolutely independent of the hand or mind of the writer. The writer, a successful businesswoman and a college graduate, had a decidedly analytical mind and is right-handed. Yet the greater part of the messages have been written with the left hand. After crossing the paper from left to right, the writing will turn from right to left, upside down. It is always clear and legible but the character of the writing changes with each individual controlling the pencil."

The messages began when the father of the family was alive in this world. (Those on the other side often protest against being called dead, saying, "We are far more alive than you are.") But when the father passed on, there was no interruption in the communication, although none has yet come from the father.

One recent automatic-writing experience occurred to one of the daughters as she sat in a room which, like the rooms in which all of this family's psychic experiences have taken place, was fully lighted. She kept a pencil in each hand, and the following messages were written simultaneously:

Left Hand	Right Hand
"You are getting a sign."	"Have patience."

As soon as the two pencils had completed their sentences a member of the family asked, "A sign of what?"

The rapidly written reply was, "Can your mind alone direct two thoughts to your fingers at one and the same time? We do it, and you on your side receive."

The written comments for that day's experiments were: "It is possible that the demonstration of simultaneous writing and the comment about it was caused by my saying early in the sitting that I wondered if I might be doing a good portion of the automatic writing with my subconscious mind. I had been made suspicious of myself because I noticed that on some days when I had noted unusual words that were new to me they would later appear in the automatic writing."

Perhaps the most significant of the comments recorded by this family are these observations that might bring help and comfort to those of us who are nagged with doubt:

"We have found the controlling influence always glad to answer any question about which they might be supposed to have knowledge. Our feeling was that they were with us and enjoying a chat with the family. Under proper physical and mental conditions I have no doubt that many can and will have the same convincing results that we have shared in our little family circle.

"The effect on all of us from the messages received has been to develop an absolute assurance of life hereafter and a degree of happiness and confidence that nothing heretofore has given us."

Occasionally investigators in this field experience a rare phenomenon which may well have some connection with the halos seen gracing the heads of saints in religious paintings. In psychic research the halo is called an aura and is defined as a shining light emanating from a person's astral body, and this in turn is defined as the spirit that survives the death of the physical body of flesh.

When halos or auras are seen they are usually witnessed by persons with strong psychic personalities and emerge from individuals who themselves are usually psychic. Often I have sat with groups of experimenters and heard the medium—such as Margery—or the spirit control—such as Walter—point out that one of us wore an aura over his head. In each instance that person had an unmistakably strong paranormal sensitivity. Usually the average person with under-developed psychic powers cannot see the aura.

My single personal experience with auras, other than the remarks I have heard at séances, took place in Brest, France, during World War I when I was a Y.M.C.A. secretary with the A.E.F. While I was stationed at Brest some French friends told me about an eight-year-old orphan girl whose father had been killed at Verdun and whose mother had died shortly thereafter.

"She is a normal child," my friends said, "except that she wears a halo in a photograph. You cannot see it yourself, but take a picture of her and it is there. No matter who takes the photograph, no matter where it is taken or how or in what kind of light, there it is. See for yourself."

I did. I prevailed upon a friend with a camera to take her picture, and I still have that snapshot—of a lovely little girl standing in front of a French shop at noon. And around her head there is a clear halo of light. I could not see it myself when I looked at the child, nor could my friend who took the picture, but for some unknown reason the camera lens could see it consistently and photographic film could record it.

If we could wrest the secret of vision from the camera lens and from the nitrates of photography, if we would open our eyes and hearts, we, too, could see the auras, and experience the wonderful revelations of the other world. We could become convinced in our minds, as well as in our hearts, that death is not the end, but the beginning of a new and more glorious experience; that life beyond the grave is a further development of our earthly schooling.

There is strong evidence that psychic power is not limited to a few extraordinary people but is latent in everyone. Sometimes this gift is recognized, but more frequently it is ignored or misunderstood. It needs to be intelligently studied, not only because any new knowledge is worth acquiring, but because of the spiritual help it can give many. As chemistry and physics are concerned with our temporal physical universe, psychic phenomena are related to an abiding spiritual universe. We are citizens of this physical world for a few short years; we will be called to be citizens of that eternal home for eternity.

We need not shut our minds to the possiblity of contacts with those who have gone over and wish to give us some sign of their survival. Our ancestors lived in a maze of what to us is superstition, and failed to examine the physical world around them. Still, to them the world of spirits was very real.

Today, as modern men, we have held our eyes so close to the eyepieces of the microscope and the telescope that we have developed a mental myopia that prevents us from seeing across the street. We have studied the physical world so assiduously that we are unable to see the spiritual world beyond.

God's power is not exhausted by our understanding of it.

8

The Mystery of Dreams

People in ancient times—perhaps because they were more superstitious and ignorant, perhaps because their simple lives were much closer to the verities—placed far more importance on dreams than we do today.

True, our modern world has its volumes of dream interpretation by modern soothsayer and modern psychiatrist alike; it has its scientists probing into the mechanics of dreams; it has its psychologists connecting dreams to the subconscious mind. But it is a rare modern man who seriously wonders if some dreams might not be simple, uncluttered communications with the psychic world.

We know that the royal courts of Babylon and Nineveh employed men whose sole job was to interpret dreams; and we read in Acts 16:9 of a divinely inspired dream—"And a vision appeared to Paul in the night: There stood a man of Macedonia, and prayed him, saying, Come over into Macedonia, and help us."—which changed St. Paul's life.

Are not some dreams psychic experiences in themselves? Few Americans are unfamiliar with the death dreams of Abraham Lincoln. This realistic, practical American repeatedly dreamed of attending his own funeral, the last time only a few days before his tragic assassination. In early April of 1865 the tall, bearded President told guests at a White House party of his previous night's dream. He was walking in the White House, he said, and suddenly became aware of the sound of weeping. He traced the voice to the East Room, where he saw mourners and guards surrounding a casket.

"Who is dead?" Lincoln asked a soldier. "The President is dead," the soldier replied. "Killed by an assassin."

A few days later, on Good Friday, April 14, the President and Mrs. Lincoln sat in a private box in Ford's Theater in Washington watching *Our American Cousin*. And it was then, during intermission, that John Wilkes Booth made Lincoln's dream of death come true.

Benjamin Franklin told friends that often his dreams had foretold the outcome of events that were of great concern to him. And Samuel Taylor Coleridge, the great English poet, composed several hundred lines of his famous poem "Kubla Khan" while dreaming during an afternoon nap. Upon awakening he immediately began to record the wonderful imagery—now not composing poetry but merely writing it from memory. He was interrupted in this task, and when he returned, the unrecorded verses had vanished, as had his dream.

I have had a somewhat similar experience, although the three verses which resulted were not written by me, nor are they of the same literary quality as "Kubla Khan."

Howard Arnold Walter is dead now—perhaps he would prefer me to say "gone to the other side"—stricken while serving as a missionary in Lahore, India. His wife and my sister Anna had been roommates in a New York City training school for Christian workers, and Howard and I became close friends. His interest in psychic forces equaled mine, and we spent long hours together in serious discussion of this subject, for both he and his wife were extremely sensitive to psychic phenomena. Howard Walter was a friend who touched my innermost being, who understood and felt my unspoken thoughts, a remarkable man, one of those rare persons to whom you really feel close in both mind and spirit.

A few years after Howard's death in India, Marion and I attended a student conference in Northfield, Massachusetts, staying in the same hotel where we had often met the Walters during similar conferences.

Dream One night, after a particularly satisfying day of accomplishment, I dreamed of Howard Walter. In the dream he sat comfortably and talked with me, and then he began to recite a poem, one that was much like those he had written when he had been alive. When the dream faded and I woke I could remember only the first line: "Who is so low that I am not his brother?" I blinked my eyes in the darkness, attempting to bring back the forgotten lines, but I failed and fell into dreamless sleep.

The following night Howard again appeared, again recited the poem, and then said, "Get up and write the words on paper."

I responded immediately. I awoke and went to the desk, rustling through the drawer for a sheet of hotel stationery. Glancing at my watch I noted it was exactly two o'clock in the morning. Marion continued to sleep as I recorded the twelve lines of verse. They flowed from my mind as easily as the ink from my fountain pen; I was not composing, I was merely recording, recalling his words from my memory and setting them down on paper. Like Coleridge with his Kubla Khan, my writing took no mental effort.

Here are the dictated words of Howard Arnold Walter:

Who is so low that I am not his brother?
    Who is so high that I've no path to him?
Who is so poor I may not feel his hunger?
    Who is so rich I may not pity him?

Who is so hurt I may not know his heartache?
    Who sings for joy my heart may never share?
Who in God's heaven has passed beyond my vision?
    Who to Hell's depths where I may never fare?

May none, then, call on me for understanding,
    May none, then, turn to me for help in pain,
And drain alone his bitter cup of sorrow,
    Or find he knocked upon my heart in vain.

This untitled "dream" poem expressed exactly the point of view that Howard held on earth; it is the same meter as one of his life-composed poems, "I Would Be True for There Are Those Who Trust Me," an inspirational verse that is well known around the world. I am sure that this dream poem was not written by S. Ralph Harlow, even half asleep, even by my subconscious in a half-dream world. I cannot help thinking that it was the personality of Harold Arnold Walter, surviving death, that gave to my mind these lines.

If dreams, or at least some of them, are indeed psychic experiences, perhaps we approach an explanation to the "I've been here before" experience that almost all of us have felt at one time or another in our lives. You are exploring a wooded path on a gentle slope in New Hampshire, and you have never been to New Hampshire before. It is pleasant and quiet, and a sense of peace lulls you into wonderful tranquility. Your senses somehow seem sharpened, and although there is not the excitement of new awareness you begin to feel that you can see more and feel more in a new perspective. Then, dimly, you begin to know that this path, this forest, this day is a timeless place and a timeless time; that you have been here before.

You are not surprised to find the split birch or the bole of the beech around the next curve of the path; you have seen them before, although you have never been there before. Do all forest paths have split birches or smooth-skinned beeches? you ask yourself in some elated confusion. And you answer: Perhaps, only perhaps, and if they do, are they always in this precise position, and would I know the pattern of the ancient lichen spattered green on the glacial boulder to my right? Yet I do; for these things I know: I have been here before, I have walked this path; yet I know that I have not. A tiny, shining facet of our minds reflects the memories of things unseen but seen, unknown but known; and somehow we are struck momentarily with a fleeting sense of the eternal.

It goes quickly, this glimpse of greater glory, but most of us have had it, regretting when it is taken back from us—sometimes snatched suddenly as if the giver changed his mind; sometimes drained slowly from our senses and leaving us again with unsatisfying reality.

Have we dreamed these experiences, these times when we recognize rooms and faces and strange places which we have never seen before, and then stored them into our subconscious for later recall? And if we have indeed dreamed them just how can we explain the precise accuracy of our dreams in foretelling what we are yet to see?

I remember a student—let's call her Anne—telling me of such a dream, a recurrent, serial-story dream, with each chapter of the experience connected to the last installment. Always the scene opened on a street corner in a small New England town. There were white-painted clapboard houses with shutters the color of ancient weathered copper. There were green lawns and lilacs and forsythia. And in each dream a young girl was waiting for her. She and Anne would chat on the corner for a moment and then stroll a hundred yards to a large old house with a huge veranda. Inside, in the big living room, a group of young people would already be gathered, and Anne and her dream companion would join them, singing around the piano, playing parlor games, and spending endless hours in young people's discussions.

Each dream was essentially a repetition of the first one; the circumstances of meeting were identical—always on the same street corner—and the stroll to the house, up the long walk to the veranda and into the living room to see the same young people gather. As the dream sequence progressed, Anne became acquainted with the other youth in the house, learned their names and characteristics, their likes and dislikes, and she became very fond of them.

And then one night, when the dream had run for perhaps a dozen nights, Anne met her friend on the corner and found her depressed and sad. "This is our last meeting," her dream friend said. "I will see you but you will not see me." Anne brushed aside the words of her friend, saying, "Of course we shall meet again." But they never did; the dreams stopped suddenly and never recurred.

A few months later, with her father and sister, who had come from Michigan for her graduation, Anne was driving up the New England coast. None of the family had ever seen the Atlantic shore, and they toured from Boston into Maine, enjoying the early summer beauty and exploring the small seacoast colonial towns.

Then suddenly in one small coastal village Anne recognized the street corner where she had met her dream friend so many times. Excitedly she said, "Father, turn left here. Turn left at this corner." And her father was obedient to his daughter's request.

"Four more houses," Anne said as they drove slowly up the street. "Three more. It's on the right just on the other side of that lilac hedge. Now. Stop here, Father. Right here. In front of this house."

Anne got out of the car. It was the house. Identical with that in her dreams. The same lilac hedge, the same four wide wooden steps to the veranda, the same huge door with tarnished brass knocker and with small rectangular panes set on each side of it. But now the lawn needed mowing and a black and white sign near the walk said "For Rent." She walked up the steps and peered into the empty building. She looked in through the bay window, past the window seat where she had sat in so many of her dreams; she saw the fireplace, empty and black now instead of dancing with flames as she had known it; and the staircase once used in her dreams as a sort of choir loft for singing youngsters. It was the house she had known, but it was empty now, its furniture gone, its floors bare and dusty, its youthful voices transferred to some other place—or to some other dreams.

In one definition of the word, Anne's dreams were consecutive; but a series of dreams would be a more accurate description, because in the literature of psychic phenomena there is a consecutive dream that involves two or more persons. In such dreams one person experiences the first part of the incident, and another takes up the dream where the first leaves off. One example of this was supplied by a former student of mine who frequently shared consecutive dreams with her mother.

The daughter reported that she dreamed she and her mother were canoeing in a swift river above a waterfall. They lost control of the canoe, and in spite of their desperate paddling they were drawn to the edge of the falls. The canoe teetered and they were swept away into the rapids below. At this point she woke, her hands clenched, her breathing heavy, her nightclothing damp with perspiration. Then she returned to sleep and spent the rest of the night in peaceful, dreamless sleep.

Next morning she told her mother, who slept in the adjoining bedroom, about her dream and was told that her mother had continued the event. Her dream had begun as she and her daughter struggled in the water at the foot of the falls, and had continued until they reached the shore, bedraggled and exhausted.

Some people have identical dreams during the same night and apparently at the same time. Dr. Hornell Hart, formerly a member of the Duke University faculty and a man who has made an exhaustive study of dreams, records one identical dream he shared with his wife. Both dreamed they walked together in the garden; he discovered their dreams were the same while describing his dream to her. He incorrectly named a flower in the dream garden, and she corrected him; then they knew that they were sharing not only their waking lives but also their dream world.

There is always the possibility that a dream can be a psychic communication with someone we have known in this life and who has gone on to the next one. Only recently my wife Marion reported to me an experience that strengthens this possibility. Marion, recovering from a broken hip, shared her hospital room with Ruth, the elderly widow of a musician.

One morning after their early hospital breakfast Ruth said, "Marion, last night I saw my husband." Marion was immediately alert because of her interest in psychic phenomena.

"It was a dream," Ruth said, "but it was so vivid. He was carrying his cornet and he played for me." Her voice softened and grew lower. "I've heard him play it many times. I recognized it. It was Chopin's 'Funeral March.' And when he'd finished he said, 'Ruth, I need you over here. Come to me.'"

And that evening Ruth, who was expected to be discharged from the hospital in a few days, did go over to her husband. She died quietly in her sleep.

I was attending a meeting in a neighboring town when I was informed of her death, and on the way home I thought of her previous night's dream and of the request made by her dead husband. At home I switched on the hall light; it burned steadily for a few minutes and then suddenly went out. It was a fairly new bulb and I remembered inserting it only a short time before. Therefore I tested it in a floor lamp. It burned brightly, and I knew I would need to call an electrician the next day to repair the hall switch, for there, obviously, was the trouble.

Then I thought of Ruth's death and our previous flashlight experience after the death of Helen, and I returned the bulb to its socket in the hall ceiling. It burned brightly and steadily. Only six hours previously I had held Ruth's hand and she had said to me in a strong voice, "I will be all right." Was the erratic light bulb just that—a manufacturer's error that escaped detection and was brought back to life by my handling of it? Or was its behavior some signal from Ruth that there is life after death—that there is survival of personality?

9

The Sixth Sense
of Telepathy

"If there *is* such a thing as the Christian spirit or soul," the skeptic has asked me a thousand times, "why is there no evidence of it? Can it be weighed? Can it be measured? Can it be photographed? Can it *do* anything?"

While I cannot supply evidence of its height and weight or its photogenic qualities, there is boundless evidence that the spirit, or the soul, or the mind—whatever we wish to call it—*can* "do" something. It can travel through space.

No longer is there any doubt about the actuality of telepathy: the ability of the mind alone to transmit messages or thoughts without the help of the five senses. In fairness this bald statement needs some explanation and some qualification. Of course there still remains some doubt—I suppose somewhere in this world there are still humans who believe that the world is flat—but the mature investigators of telepathy are no longer working on the problem of *whether* it exists; they have shifted to studies of when and how and why it exists. The first hurdle of the study seems to have been cleared rather cleanly.

And now once we accept the existence and the actuality of telepathy do we not reach a second plane of inquiry? Can we not now ask if this sixth sense is evidence of spiritual man as opposed to physical man? And then can we not ask if spiritual man survives what we call death?

Whether further research will label telepathy as psychic, paranormal, or psychological—and it *will* be labeled, for modern man insists that even his ideas be labeled as large as the contents of his medicine cabinet—is not important to us now. Its existence is important; its meaning even more so.

As perhaps most humans have, throughout my life I have frequently brushed against telepathy. And although I never cease to be struck with wonder about it, it somehow does not seem so mysterious as other phenomena which we toss into the same bin labeled parapsychological. Perhaps it is because it is not so much more wondrous than radio, radar, and television transmission; perhaps we secretly feel that there *should* be such a thing as telepathy, and our secret feeling makes us accept it more easily.

And perhaps it is because we are all born of woman and we have been subjected to the peculiar telepathy of females in ordinary conversation.

"What time did you—?" Mrs. P. asks her daughter, not completing the sentence because she knows it is unnecessary for the needs of communication.

"Before ten, Mother," the daughter responds.

"Did you have—?"

"Wonderful. Absolutely wonderful. I thought he'd forgotten, but—"

"Yes, I know, dear. I saw it in the refrigerator."

"Isn't it fabulous? My first orchid!"

"Your father and I planned to—"

"Oh, I know, Mother, but you were so tired. You don't need to wait up for me any more. After all, I'm—"

"Yes, you are. And soon you'll—"

"Mother, do you think Aunt May—"

"Of course, dear. Your Aunt May wouldn't think of missing your graduation."

And so it goes, and probably always has gone. Women are the skilled practitioners of this art of cryptic conversation, although some men have acquired the faculty. In fact some of the nation's most prominent scientists, some working on Information Theory, play a lunchtime game that demonstrates how many useless words we use in conversation, using them despite the fact that the meaning of the sentence already has been made clear. Here is an example, with the obvious words deleted:

"Hello, John, how are——?"

"Just——, and——?"

"Pretty——."

"How's the——?"

"About the——."

"Well, I hope she gets——. Give her my——, will——?"

Now of course this is not telepathy, but the fact that we can, and do, frequently communicate without words makes telepathy a little less strange to us.

One of the most interesting and most closely controlled telepathic experiments I have observed took place in Athens one winter, when I was teaching there on sabbatical leave from Smith College.

The Greek Society of Psychical Research, which at that time limited its membership to university teachers and other professional men and women, was conducting a series of telepathic experiments jointly with groups at the University of Paris and the University of Berlin. The president of the Greek Society was one of the nation's most prominent surgeons, a man well trained in the investigation of psychic phenomena, and the men and women who sat around that table with me were among the ablest minds of Greece. Few of them were interested in religion or immortality—in fact some of them were atheists—but all were vitally concerned with telepathy. They wanted to test the phenomena with scientific methods of procedure.

When I joined the group in that winter of 1930-31 the experiments had already been in progress for many weeks. There had been some failures, some partial failures, and some remarkable successes in sending and receiving information transmitted only by telepathy the eleven hundred miles to Berlin and the thirteen hundred miles to Paris.

The method was quite simple and the same procedure was followed at each of the weekly meetings. At each meeting three of us were selected to bring three different objects to the following week's get-together. Their identity was to be revealed to the other members only when the circle met at the appointed hour. I remember bringing an egg the night another professor brought a pair of scissors and a local doctor produced a medical book. This was on a night when it was the Athens group's turn to act as transmitter. On other nights, along with either Berlin or Paris, we acted as receivers.

Our official watch already had been synchronized by telephone with the other university groups, and at the appointed time the sending began and lasted for exactly ten minutes. As a sender we used a young woman with highly developed and previously tested telepathic powers. Because women seem to be more telepathically sensitive, the other groups also had women sitting with them as receivers.

Only minutes before the experiment was to begin we produced the articles we had been commissioned to bring to the circle. They were placed under bright light in the center of the large round table around which we sat, and this was the first time that the other members knew what we had brought. Then the Greek surgeon placed the young woman in a hypnotic trance. When another member nodded to him that the precise time had been reached he said slowly and clearly, "On the table is an egg, a white egg, a chicken's egg. It is a white egg. There is also a pair of scissors, a pair of shears, used for cutting cloth or paper, a pair of scissors. And there is a book, an ordinary book, a book of normal size."

After he had described the objects several times he said, "You are to send a picture of these three objects to two persons who are waiting to receive the picture. One is in Paris; the other is in Berlin. They will get your thought vibrations."

In Berlin and Paris the scene was quite similar as the separate research societies attempted to receive the pictures that our young woman was attempting to send. Already their young women had been placed in hypnotic trance and had been told that three pictures were being sent to them from Athens. And in darkened rooms for ten minutes there was silence as the receiving groups waited for the transmission time to end.

At the end of the allotted time the three telepathic sensitives were brought out of their trances. We at the sending end in Athens would then draw three identical, simple, outline sketches of the objects on the table: in the case of this experiment, drawings of an egg, a pair of scissors, and a book. One of these drawings would be pasted into a large record book with space left on the page for the drawings that would be sent us from Berlin and Paris.

Meanwhile the groups in France and Germany were already watching their sensitives draw pictures of what they had mentally received during the ten-minute hypnotic trance. Two copies would be made; one would be sent to us in Athens for our record book, the other mailed to the third group of investigators.

Then eagerly we would wait for the mail to bring us evidence of triumph or failure. Sometimes there was nothing from both of the receivers and we would be disappointed, wondering if the human mind, like a radio set, could be blanked out by some equivalent of sunspots, cosmic radiation, or aurora borealis. Sometimes we would get drawings that indicated only partial reception, and there were experiments when Berlin, for example, would receive perfectly but Paris was blank or imperfect.

But there were also the times when almost identical drawings were received and were placed side by side with the drawing we had made in Athens in almost perfect triplication; and these were the exciting times. We never learned how to control our experiments or the reasons for either success or failure, and we could never make even an intelligent beforehand guess about that night's potential success; but time after time we proved the power of mind over space. Never have I witnessed such positive proof of the actuality of telepathy.

But even greater distances were spanned, and even more conclusive evidence gathered, in the famous experiments conducted a few years later by Sir Hubert Wilkins, the hardened, practical polar explorer, and Harold M. Sherman, a New York author.

On August 12, 1937, a Russian aviator named Sigismund Levanevsky and five companions took off from Moscow on a transpolar flight to the United States with a first stop planned at Fairbanks, Alaska. Their route had already been successfully tracked by two previous Russian planes, but these had been especially constructed long-range aircraft. Levanevsky was commanding a conventional, multimotored plane, and his purpose was to demonstrate the feasibility of transpolar flight with normal aircraft.

But his demonstration was a tragic failure and his plane has never been found. Somewhere between the North Pole and Alaska, Levanevsky was forced down, with only an erratic, static-stuttering radio message to give a hint of his position. Four days after the plane crash-landed, Sir Hubert Wilkins volunteered to lead a group to find the downed fliers.

The primary purpose of the Wilkins expedition, of course, was to rescue the Russian fliers or find their bodies. But before leaving, Sir Hubert made arrangements with Harold Sherman to conduct a long series of telepathic experiments. Sherman had become interested in telepathy some years before, had discovered that he himself was sensitive to such communications, and had occasionally discussed the subject with Wilkins. The polar explorer was not much intrigued with psychic phenomena—in fact they somewhat repelled him—but as a boy in Australia he had been impressed with the knowledge of the aborigines about unexpected events which they could not possibly have known through normal means but which were actually taking place miles beyond their range of sight or hearing. As he later wrote, Wilkins was "interested in the possibility of dependable and willed thought transference from one living individual to another."

His arrangement with Sherman was that three times each week, on Monday, Tuesday, and Thursday, at 11:30 P.M. Eastern Standard Time, he would spend thirty minutes attempting to transmit his thoughts. Sherman would attempt to receive the thoughts in his Riverside Drive apartment, and Wilkins would "send" from wherever he was at the appointed times—from Arctic Canada, from Alaska, or while flying over the barren floes of the Arctic Ocean. In the five months of the experiment, from October 25, 1935, to March 23, 1935, Sherman sat for sixty-eight test "receptions." Not always was the polar aviator available, or even willing, to carry out the experiments—he admits slacking on the job several times—but Sherman never missed an appointment.

Sherman recorded the images that came to his mind each night, and they came regularly, even when Wilkins was not consciously "sending," and the record indicates that Sherman was reading Wilkins' mind. Because of magnetic and sunspot disturbances the New York *Times* radio operator in New York who was assigned to keep in contact with the Wilkins party during the search managed to communicate with the searchers only thirteen times in the five-month period; Sherman made sixty-eight contacts, and later when his notes were compared to Wilkins' diary they contained an amazing number of "hits" that could not be explained by imagination, coincidence, or educated guesses.

For sixty-eight nights Harold Sherman sat for thirty minutes in his darkened study concentrating on the thoughts of a man three thousand miles away, and his reception was remarkable. After each session he would type his notes and mail two copies of them—one to a Columbia University professor of psychology whose integrity was above reproach, and the other to the New York *Times* radio operator assigned to contact the Wilkins rescue party. This was to assure the integrity of Sherman himself.

While the rest of the world did not know, Sherman was the only man, other than Wilkins or the members of his expedition, who knew the intimate details of the party's daily work and many of Wilkins' personal and unspoken thoughts. Sherman knew when Wilkins' plane was damaged (he wrote specifically and accurately, "a crack in the tail of the fuselage"); he knew when Wilkins saw the body of a sled dog, shot through the head, on the banks of the Mackenzie River; when Wilkins watched Eskimo women fishing through the ice at Point Barrow; when a pair of heavy boots needed repair; even when Wilkins twice rejected money offers for the endorsement of American whiskies.

After reviewing the published reports of the five-month experiments Dr. J. B. Rhine wrote from Duke University, "It represents a contribution to the study of Extrasensory Perception...for even the psychologist interested in ESP will doubtless find himself...willing to accept the findings as certainly suggestive and be reasonably well satisfied that this was actually transmission of thought through space without any known means of communication."

And the *Times* radio operator, who had been frankly skeptical about the tests and had called them "a pretty screwy business," testified: "...Sherman actually had a more accurate telepathic knowledge of what was happening to Wilkins in his search for the lost Russian fliers than I was able to gain in my ineffective attempts to keep in touch by short-wave radio."

I once conducted a similar experiment, much more modest in terms of duration and distance, with a friend who was then secretary of the Congregational Mission Board in Boston. Dr. Ruth Seabury, coincidentally a Smith alumna, was a prominent leader in young people's conferences, the author of several books, and an intelligent and sincere investigator of psychical phenomena.

Our plan ran almost parallel to the Wilkins-Sherman tests. We agreed to attempt contact at ten o'clock for six consecutive nights; I was to be the sender, she the receiver. She was to go to her room in Boston at the appointed time and sit in the dark, concentrating on any message or picture that I might be able to transmit. I was in Northampton, just about one hundred miles away as the crow—and a telepathic message—flies.

The first test night was a Monday, and as was my habit I was engaged in evening study when ten o'clock chimed. So deeply engrossed, in fact, that it was not until ten minutes after the hour that I suddenly remembered our agreement. Quickly then I extinguished all the lights in the study except for one large table lamp, and I sat quietly, staring at it, concentrating on it, willing with all my strength that a picture of that lamp be transmitted to Miss Seabury in Boston.

After about ten minutes of this concentration I drew a picture of the lamp, wrote a letter explaining that I had been late in attempting transmission and apologizing for my tardiness. I sealed the letter immediately and mailed it a few minutes later in the post box near our home.

The next day I received a letter from Miss Seabury. Our letters had crossed in the mails, and she had not yet received mine. With the letter was a drawing of a lamp, almost identical with the one I had sent to her and which she had not seen when she had mailed her letter to me. She wrote: "I went to my room at ten o'clock and sat in complete darkness. Nothing happened for at least ten minutes, so I decided that the experiment was a failure and was about to turn on the electric light. Suddenly I had a distinct picture of a lamp in my mind as on a white screen. I sat down and the picture remained clear. So I enclose a drawing. I shall be interested to hear from you."

On those six nights of experiment we scored four out of six possible "hits," a performance which baseball writers would describe as a .667 batting average and which in cold, hard statistics takes it out of the area of coincidence.

Our two failures might be explained by the circumstances of transmission. The first occurred on a night when my wife and I were attending a play at a local theater. Our seats were in the balcony and we were surrounded with laughing, talking college students. Transmission time, ten o'clock, came between acts, and in the noise and confusion I sat in my seat and attempted to get through to Miss Seabury. That night she received nothing.

The second failure took place on a rainy night when at ten o'clock I was walking down the street following a man holding an umbrella over his head. I concentrated on the umbrella, but even my own visual sense, operating through my eyes, transmitted a fluctuating image to my brain. At times the object was in deep shadow, and then again it would be in the bright glare of a street light. This night, too, was a blank to Miss Seabury.

Other than knowing that telepathy is an actuality, we really know very little about it. We do not know just how Sherman received his messages from Wilkins three thousand miles away; we do not know just how I sent the picture of the lamp to Miss Seabury a hundred miles away. As with many other fields of investigation our ignorance about telepathy is indeed profound. But some of the best, most reliable, and most consistent work on the subject is being done by Dr. J. B. Rhine, a psychologist who heads Duke University's Parapsychology Laboratory in Durham, North Carolina.

He started with a simple thesis. During one of my first visits to him he told me, "I had studied many psychic experiences, hundreds of them, perhaps thousands. Many of them did not bear up under investigation; they were not genuine. But a large residue remained. These seemed undoubtedly authentic, actual cases that were actual fact. And if these cases *were* genuine then the mind of man has the power to acquire knowledge and to transmit information apart and not dependent upon the five senses. This is what I have been studying."

Best known of Dr. Rhine's work are his several decades of telepathic experiments with his famous ESP cards. These are especially printed, about the size of ordinary bridge cards, and come twenty-five cards to a set. Imprinted on them are five simple symbols—a circle, a square, a star, a cross that resembles an arithmetical plus sign, and a set of waving lines. A deck contains five of each of these cards.

Rhine has been using the ESP deck to see if, and to what extent, man can transmit or receive information through the powers of the mind alone. Now the mathematical laws of chance tell us quite accurately and precisely that if we simply *guess* which of five face-down cards is imprinted with a star—while the other four are differently imprinted—our chances are one in five. Therefore any continued guessing over a long period of time must result in a score of 20 per cent, plus or minus a minute fraction, or a score of twenty out of a possible perfect score of one hundred.

But Dr. Rhine has found subjects who consistently score in the thirties, a performance with a staggering defiance of statistical chance. Some of his more sensitive subjects have "guessed" scores so high that the odds against their records were 4,000,000 to one. Now, of course, events do happen despite the mathematical odds against them. People *do* draw thirteen spades in a bridge game. But this sort of mathematical lightning rarely strikes twice in the same bridge game and almost never is consistent in its visits to one person. Yet Rhine has found individuals who seem to be the source of telepathic bolts which strike repeatedly and consistently.

The early Rhine experiments with the ESP deck received criticism about method. At that time two persons, one a transmitter and the other a receiver, sat at a desk with a face-down deck of ESP cards in front of them. Systematically the person transmitting would look at the top card and attempt to send its image—a circle or cross or waving line or star or square—to the receiver opposite him. But, some critics pointed out, the printing of the cards might have embossed them, so that an outline of their images might be seen on the blank side. Today Rhine separates his experimenters, either by placing a screen between them so that the receiver cannot see the cards or by placing them yards and sometimes miles apart in different rooms and buildings. The fantastic results have not been altered.

On my most recent visit to Duke to see Dr. Rhine I observed machines shuffling the cards and I again took a turn at the cards. Over the years I have been fairly consistent in my scoring, and this time I was no different. I scored thirty out of a hundred—four runs through the pack—which is an indication that I happen to be particularly sensitive to this type of telepathy.

But actually, at least to me, Rhine's ESP decks and his experiments with telepathy do not in themselves have a great deal of significance, unless they are interpreted in a broader sense. Once I mentioned this reservation to him. "I'm not much interested in these card games and whether ESP can prove that the mind reaches beyond the limits of physical energy. As a minister I am concerned with whether we discover any proof that the affirmations we make by faith are supported by facts."

Dr. Rhine smiled at me. "Dr. Harlow," he said, "that is exactly what I am interested in proving."

Although, as Dr. Rhine points out in one of his books, "the resources of skepticism are almost infinite," and as Jesus said, "although one rose from the dead, they would not believe," the evidence for ESP as accumulated by Dr. Rhine and other investigators points to a nonphysical or spiritual factor in the human personality.

For me the proof which telepathy offers is significant in this respect: if the mind is wholly dependent on a physical brain in order to express or experience consciousness and memory, the dissolution of the physical brain (death) would mean the end of all conscious existence. This is the theory held by the humanists. But all through history, back of the days of primitive man, humans have felt deep within them that they are built on the scale of two worlds, not one. All the great philosophers, from the Golden Age of Greece to the present day, have asserted that man is not simply flesh, that he is also spirit, and that while flesh is mortal and temporal, spirit is immortal and eternal.

As William James often told us in class, while we are in these physical bodies we need to make use of the physical brain to express the *thoughts* of the mind, but it cannot be disproved that mind will be able to express itself far better through some other means, once we are freed from the "body of this death," as St. Paul puts it.

To me telepathy is proof that the mind is *not* dependent upon the physical brain for the transmission of thoughts through space. This has a most significant bearing on prayer and on all mystical experiences in which the presence of God is felt, as so well expressed in Alfred Tennyson's "The Higher Pantheism."

> Speak to Him thou for He hears,
> and Spirit with Spirit can meet—
> Closer is He than breathing, and
> nearer than hands and feet.

10

Warnings from the Other Side

As soon as I saw them sitting there near the front of the church, listening to my Easter Sunday sermon, I said to myself, "Now I'm in for it. I know exactly what they'll say when the service is over."

At its beginning my sermon had been fairly typical, the kind that many ministers preach on that day—inspirational and advancing the reasons that any convinced Christian would use in defense of the claims of St. Paul.

As acting minister during weekends of All Souls Church in Lowell, Massachusetts, a union of Congregationalists and Unitarians, I had preached on the text from the Book of Job—"If a man die, shall he live again?"; and from St. Paul's letter to the church in Corinth—"As we have born the image of the earthly, we shall also bear the image of the heavenly." Then I had expanded into my thesis about the conservation of energy, saying that it is unthinkable that God planned to conserve only material things, that He planned to have the personality of man, the spiritual values, erode into nothingness along with his physical body.

And toward the end I discussed spiritual experiences and revelations and spoke of Jesus and His life as a living God and man's witness to immortality. It was natural that I mention psychical research and the accumulating evidence supporting faith in survival. And I recounted two of my own psychic experiences—the cracking of the glass inkwell and the mysterious flashlight incident.

It was then that I became conscious of Reverend Charles Joy, my classmate at Harvard, and his wife sitting in the front pew. Dr. Joy was a former minister of All Souls. I felt sure I would be reproved by him for including the paranormal in my Easter sermon.

As I approached the Joys at the end of the sermon I said, "Now, Charlie, I know what you're going to say, but this—"

He interrupted, smiling at me. "Not at all, not at all. Far from it. My wife and I have had experiences more amazing than the ones you just mentioned. In fact we have been interested in psychic phenomena for many years as a result of our own experiences."

But the Joys had something to say, and we sat for more than an hour on one of the front pews, completely forgetting about lunch as we talked, and they told me dozens of personal psychic experiences, many of them concerning apparitions. Two of them are of particular interest, involving warnings of death and danger from Mrs. Joy's mother, who had died several years earlier.

"Father was alive then," Mrs. Joy said, "living about fifty miles away with my sister. Charles was out of the house that morning—perhaps making pastoral calls, but I don't remember. I do remember it was a bright sunny day and I was alone in the house. I started upstairs and when I looked up, there was Mother standing at the top of the stairs, looking down at me, smiling, saying nothing, apparently waiting for me. I was a little startled, of course, but not astonished, for she had appeared to me before.

"I continued on up the stairs, getting closer and closer to Mother, until I was as near her as I am to you now. I tried to see through her, but she seemed to have solid substance and appeared younger and more beautiful than when I last saw her in the flesh. Continuing to smile, she said, quite distinctly, 'Your father is coming over here in a few days, and you ought to know it.' Then she was gone."

When Dr. Joy returned home later that morning and heard of his wife's experience he said, "Perhaps you'd better go see your father. You'd feel better, wouldn't you?" She agreed, and that afternoon took the train to her sister's home.

Her father was out for an afternoon walk when she arrived, and Mrs. Joy and her sister talked about the apparition. Her sister said, "But Father is in perfect health; he's never looked better." Nevertheless she agreed that a thorough physical examination would relieve them both, and arranged for it that afternoon. The family physician reported, "He's in splendid condition for his age. I can find nothing physically wrong with him."

Mrs. Joy stayed overnight with her sister and father and the next morning returned to her home in Lowell, somewhat puzzled about her mother's message but confident about the health of her father. As she opened the front door the telephone was ringing. It was her sister, reporting that their father had just died of a sudden heart attack.

Now there are certain aspects of this experience which challenge the mind. There is no indication of telepathy; no person concerned, not even the doctor, had the slightest evidence that death was near. Mrs. Joy had had no premonition of her father's approaching death, for if she had she would not have returned home so quickly, thinking that her rush visit was a wild-goose chase. Yet her mother's message had been impelling enough to send her on the visit; and as events showed, it was accurate.

Without being dogmatic, and reserving the thought that there might be some other explanation of this experience, let me suggest an interpretation that does not seem unreasonable to me.

Just as I was writing about this experience my telephone rang and at the other end of the line was a person who said he was my six-year-old grandson. Now I could not see him, but I accept this assertion on the sound of his voice and on his message which gave me certain information which I am able to check. Previous experiences assure me that it is reasonable to suppose that the voice I heard was my grandson's. But my only actual proof lies in my familiarity with his voice, in the nature of his message, and in my ability to check the information he gave me. Of course many such experiences enter into my conclusion that it was indeed my grandson who spoke to me.

Now let us suppose that there are intelligences who have information thus far unavailable to those of us on earth, especially knowledge that relates to contacts between this world and the world beyond. In a rational universe it would not seem unreasonable that a man's wife would be among the first to be given knowledge that her husband was about to join her in what can best be described as heaven. Mrs. Joy's mother—knowing that her daughter had psychic ability, having appeared to her several times in the past—would naturally communicate her information to her daughter. I find nothing unreasonable in this explanation of the experience.

Another time, Mrs. Joy told me, her mother saved her life, or at least saved her from harm and injury. Mrs. Joy was staying in a house unfamiliar to her; she was sleeping soundly and had gone to bed with no premonitions. During the night she was wakened by a touch on her head. It was a gentle but firm touch, and she was immediately awake. Her mother was standing by the bed. "Come, dear," she said. "Follow me." Her mother took Mrs. Joy's hand and guided her into the hall. There Mrs. Joy knew why her mother had wakened her: the hall was filled with choking smoke; the house was on fire. In a few minutes her mother had guided Mrs. Joy through unfamiliar hallways and stairs to safety. Then she vanished.

Another and more dramatic incident of a living person being saved from danger by a relative who has passed on was told me in Greece by the widow of Tom, the spirit who so beautifully illuminated the wall of our basement dining room.

"It was soon after Tom's death," Virginia told us. "I was driving home late one night down a narrow street, and suddenly in front of me there was a pair of weaving headlights, careening from one side of the road to the other. The driver was obviously very, very drunk. There was no time to dodge, and even if there had been I could not know which way to turn. To say I was frightened is an understatement; I was simply overcome with fear and resigned to the inevitable collision. I just hoped it would not be too severe. And then you know what I did? I just dropped my hands into my lap. Yes. I simply gave up. It might not make any sense, but that's what I did.

"And then I felt a tap on my left shoulder, just like the taps that Tom would give me when he was here and we would be out together and I would be driving with him next to me with his arm over the back of the seat. It was just like that, a slight tap that had meant, 'Watch out, dear.' Then the wheel straightened out, as if Tom were steering the car, and we passed the other auto by the skin of my teeth, just squeaking by. I was not steering, for I remember looking into my lap and seeing my hands lying there, lifeless, palms up, as if they were not a part of me at all.

"The car took *me* home. I didn't steer it. The same hands that had avoided a head-on collision retained command of the wheel and even guided it into the driveway. I did step on the brake pedal and the car stopped. And when I was there, stopped and safe again, I felt another tap on my shoulder, and that was all. I know who it was. I haven't the slightest doubt that it was Tom. And I was so glad—not only to be saved from that horrible accident but also to know that Tom is all right, and still loves me, and still takes care of me."

It seems almost ridiculous to say that death—or the passing on into another world, whichever it is—is of supreme importance to the living. But it seems less ridiculous to say so when we recognize that most psychic experiences are closely connected, in both time and space, with death. Often the human personality that has survived death desires to communicate almost immediately with those he left behind, and quite frequently he succeeds. For example a student told me about the time of her grandfather's death.

My student—let's call her Sally—was sitting at home in front of the fireplace with her mother when they both heard a loud rapping at the front door. Her mother went into the hall to answer the door, and turned on the porch light, but no one was there. She looked about on the porch, shrugged, and returned. Her daughter asked, "Who was it?" The mother replied, "No one. We must be hearing things."

She had hardly seated herself when the knock was repeated, this time much more loudly. Sally said, "It's some prankster. Don't pay any attention to it, Mother." But Sally's mother answered again, and again no one was there.

When the knock came the third time, almost immediately, they both went to the door and found no one. Then Sally's mother said, "I wonder if anything has happened to Father."

She immediately telephoned her mother in a nearby city. She talked for only a few minutes, then hung up the receiver and said to Sally, "Your grandfather died only a few minutes ago. A sudden heart attack."

Is this indeed a sort of signal from the spirit world? The voluminous literature of the phenomena indicates that it is. Flammarion records many such cases, and my own files contain dozens of similar incidents. For example a Smith College housemother, a woman of marked intelligence and common sense told me of an experience she witnessed. Mrs. Smith, as we shall call her, spent her summers in a small New England village not far from Northampton. There she became acquainted with the elderly son of David G. Farragut, the great Civil War admiral, and with his family who were also summer residents.

In the middle of one summer the old man died, hardly unexpectedly at his age, but the unexpected happened the day after his demise. About noon a long-distance call came in from San Francisco.

An elderly man, a retired Navy officer who identified himself as an old friend of the dead man's, asked, "Is Farragut there?"

"Who? No," a relative answered and started to report his death, but the old friend interrupted.

"Well, where is he? He called me yesterday and we'd barely started talking when the line went dead. I haven't heard from him in years. At first I thought he was here in San Francisco, but he hadn't said when the line went dead."

"He called you yesterday?" the relative asked.

"Why, yes. Of course he did. I know his voice and was talking to him."

"Are you sure it was he?"

"Of course I'm sure. He called me by my nickname. There are few persons alive who know my nickname. Farragut knows it. Is he there?"

"Forgive me," the relative answered. "But this is important. What time did he call you?"

The old naval officer told them and then transposed the time to Eastern Daylight Time. "It couldn't be," the relative replied. "It couldn't be."

"Well, maybe it couldn't be," Farragut's friend replied with some impatience, "but it was. After we were cut off I telephoned every place in the whole San Francisco area where he might be. Even the hospitals."

"I'm sorry to tell you this," the relative replied, "but he couldn't have telephoned you. He died last evening approximately three hours before you received that call."

A similar case, in which I personally know the persons involved, happened recently. In this instance a young woman answered the telephone to hear her husband's voice clearly say only one word, "Good-by." And then the phone was dead. A short time later she was informed that her husband had died of a heart attack shortly after reaching his office. When she compared the time of his death with the time of the telephone message from her husband, she found that she had received the call about thirty minutes after her husband had died.

And in my own family I have an instance of a premonition of death. Shortly before he died my nephew Dr. William R. Birge, my sister Anna's son, visited Marion and me with his wife and baby son. We were very close, Bill and I, and he, too, had a highly developed interest in psychic experiences. As a result of my suggestion he studied under Dr. Rhine at Duke University, and we often discussed many phases of the paranormal. His wife told me that as they drove away from our house after that last visit with us he turned to her and said, "I have a strange feeling that I shall never see Uncle Ralph and Aunt Marion again on earth." Not much later he passed on, bringing his premonition to actuality. His visit was the last time he saw us.

We live in an age in which many of us have lost faith in a life beyond. Too many of us feel that man is merely a higher form of brute, recently emerged from the jungle, and with no divine touch with the Infinite.

True, we have gained something by not being motivated, as were our fathers, by the promise of a golden crown in a perfect hereafter or by the dreadful terror of the hot fires of hell. But the age itself has changed us even more. Our militarism, our leap from earth-bound lives to space exploration, has reduced our faith in immortality; often mankind seems determined to march toward chaos and destruction.

Yet in spite of all this, in spite of the explanations of nuclear and solid-state physicists, there seems to be an awakening desire for some spiritual explanation of the universe. With each new discovery of its vastness and its agelessness the universe becomes more mysterious and less understandable. Its explanation can come only from the One who planned these wonders and who can guide our rocket ships as they venture into space.

It may yet be proved that psychical research, with its eventual solutions of Farragut's telephone call and Mrs. Joy's contacts with her mother, will open the doors to renewed faith, renewed conviction as to the value of man, and a new respect for life.

11

The Experience of Dying

More than fifty years ago when I was a college student I spent my summer vacation months as a door-to-door book salesman. And, as I have been all my life, I was more interested in people than in money. The result was that I met and got to know many interesting persons, and I quickly became familiar with the problems that beset us all.

I remember one morning when I called on a young mother in Spencer, Massachusetts. I sold her no books, but when she learned I was a theology student we chatted about the perplexities of life, and I joined her over a cup of coffee in the kitchen, and then I played some hymns on the small organ in her living room.

It was after we had sung several hymns that she began to unburden herself, hoping that I could help her. Only recently, she told me, her little three-year-old daughter had died. She had adjusted reasonably well to her loss, but she broke down in tears and wept as she said, "I know she is all right now; I know I'll see her in heaven. But I don't want to see my little girl as a grown woman. I want to see her as she was when I saw her last."

I could not comfort her then but I think I could now. Psychical research has helped.

Some years after this incident, while I was attending a séance, I contacted a woman who had died in her eighties and who had also lost a little girl of three. And she, too, when she had been in this life, had worried that she might not know her little daughter when her own time came to pass on.

"But when I came here to what you call heaven," she said, "I found my little girl and she was unchanged. She was still three years old and she was even wearing the little blue dress that I had made for her."

The little girl ran to her mother and jumped into her arms and cried, "Mother!" in the voice her mother had known more than half a century before when they had both been on this earth.

Then the mother pushed her little daughter away from her and looked her in the eyes and said, "But, child, you've been here for fifty years or more; you can't remain the same!"

The child replied, "No, Mother, but I knew you'd remember me this way and would want to see me this way. Here we can be seen as we wish to be seen." And later this child was seen by her mother in other stages of normal growth.

Our curiosity about the precise nature of the hereafter is equal to our curiosity, and frequently our trepidation about the precise nature of getting to this hereafter. These two questions—what is death? and what is heaven?—have been with us in some form or other ever since there has been mankind. The answers are not so sharp and clear as we would like, but nearly eighty years of conservative research into the paranormal have given us some hints, some glimpses, some fleeting flashes of the future, some surprises, and a great deal of comfort.

The literature on these two subjects repeatedly records irritation on the part of those who have passed on when we use the words "dead" and "heaven." "We are not dead," they say. "We are more alive than you are; we have simply passed along, or progressed, to another stage." They are more tolerant regarding the word "heaven" but they say, "You have an incorrect concept of it, and we can explain it only partially, but the word itself gives a wrong impression."

However, for the sake of discussion here we will use the words "death" and "dead" and "heaven" simply because it is more practical for us to do so.

What happens at death? What do we really experience when we die? All of us will learn this for ourselves one day, through personal experience, but few of us are content to wait for this eventual knowledge. We want to know beforehand; we are impatient; and many of us are filled with fear.

But apparently there is no need for fear. When death comes painlessly or suddenly, as it so often does, the surviving personality (or the astral body, if we accept this phrase), now free of the flesh, is not at first aware of the transition. This is reported again and again by those who have gone through the change. They are confused and puzzled over much that has happened. A soldier, killed in combat by a shell explosion, will attempt to help his comrades carry in his own shattered body. A woman suddenly finds herself standing by her bed and walks downstairs and wonders why her loved ones do not seem to see her.

On the other hand there are deaths that are painful and prolonged, calling for fortitude and patience. When a person has endured much suffering or a long illness the transition seems to be of another character. In such cases there is evidently a period of rest, even of deep sleep, in which the person is not aware of survival or existence. The awakening in the other world comes gradually, often in another environment, such as a lovely countryside, where the newborn spirit finds himself lying on the bank of a brook surrounded by green fields and flowers.

Generally a friendly spirit is nearby, waiting to introduce the new spirit into the heavenly country. And as in sudden death the new spirit is often not aware that a transition—death—has taken place. Memories of the final hours come back and the astral self dreads a return to the painful life in his physical body. And now the spirit guide, perhaps a relative or loved one who has preceded the newborn spirit, will give assurance and confidence. This type of experience has been recorded in many messages.

In some cases it would seem that dying can be a more pleasant experience than birth, for psychologists tell us that many babies do not want to be born, and the assertion seems to make sense. The environment within the mother before birth was more comfortable, the method of nourishment more satisfactory than that in the world outside, and the unborn had greater security. And they protest against being born. For some of them, the psychologists say, this attitude continues for weeks, and only love and constant attention to their wants lure them into accepting this world.

But if this is true for some of us it can give us only academic comfort, for we do not remember it. Birth is behind us; it is done, and if we protested our entry into this world we do not know it. It is the next great transition that is important to us.

One message from a departed person, and recorded by a close friend of mine, says death "is more a passing through an inanimate barrier than the breaking of stretched cord. When normal, death is a pleasant experience. Passing through shock is more difficult and takes longer recuperation."

It sounds so much like the experience of dreaming, or recovering from an illness with a high fever. And the more specific, detailed descriptions of dying, by those who have experienced this transition, sound even more like dreams. Take the death of Louise Andrews, for example.

Louise was an unselfish, devoted Christian after whom a girls' camp has been named at Northfield, Massachusetts. She had been a very close friend of Marguerite and Howard Walter's—the same Howard Walter who was so dear to me and who dictated verse to me after his death—and it was the Walters to whom she came after her own painful death.

It was while the Walters were living in India that Louise contacted them. One evening while sitting quietly at home Marguerite Walter felt a sudden urge to write; she felt a force guiding her right arm and she could not control it. Her fingers picked up a pencil and her husband handed her a sheet of paper. At first her hand made large circles on the paper and then it began to write the words "Mary wants to write." This sentence was repeated several times before words began to flow in orderly sequence. "Mary"—a spirit purporting to be a girl recently emancipated from her earthly body and still confused in her new environment—was only the first of several visiting intelligences from the other side who wrote hundreds of pages of automatic writing through Marguerite Walter.

Then one day Louise Andrews, their old and dear friend, began to come through. I learned from Louise's father that she had died of cancer of the throat, but this was after I heard from Marguerite and Howard Walter what Louise had reported about her own death.

"My last memory of earth," she wrote through Marguerite Walter's hand, "was lying in bed with my family around me. Some of them were weeping. The pain in my throat was worse—much worse—and I could not get air. I could not breathe. Then suddenly the pain was gone and I was lying on the bank of a beautiful brook beneath a huge tree that cast its shade over me.

"Standing near me and watching me was a man dressed in white. I had never seen him before but I immediately felt his friendship and his calmness and his goodness. He asked me if I felt strong enough to take a walk. I did not know, for I had just awakened. But I noticed immediately that I could breathe without pain. And I rose and walked toward him, and found that I could walk, but I wondered about the body I was then in, for although it was very real it seemed so different from the body of flesh.

"I began to fear this was a dream, for if it was I knew I would wake into a world of pain again, and I did not want any more pain. Then I remembered my last earthly memory and my mother beside my bed weeping, and I looked at my guide with some sort of new understanding. I was struck by the beauty of the countryside, and I saw a group of persons strolling through the field, singing as they walked.

"I asked my companion, 'Is this heaven?' and he replied, 'That is what some call it, my dear.' And then I knew."

Another spirit who contacted this world through Marguerite Walter was a German army officer who had been killed in World War I while attempting to bring back one of his wounded men, a youth from his home town in Germany. When the German commanded Marguerite's hand he wrote in broken English with much German mixed into his messages. I studied this German officer's writing and his development over a period of many months, and most significant to me was his steady growth in spiritual perception, which gave me some insight about the workings of what we call heaven. Of course I had already been impressed with the way he had died, for I was reminded of the words of Jesus, "Greater love hath no man than this, that a man lay down his life for his friends."

But one of the most interesting descriptions of death came to Marguerite through Miner Rogers, a missionary who had been Howard Walter's roommate at both Princeton and Hartford Theological Seminary. Rogers had been assigned to Turkey as a missionary and had been killed in the terrible Adana massacre by the Turks. When Miner Rogers contacted Marguerite Walter both Howard and Marguerite knew of Miner's death, but they had never been told the details of that day.

The story, as told by the dead missionary through automatic writing to Marguerite Walter, told of the day of the massacre when the mission compound was being attacked by the Turks. Miner told of carrying a pail of water down a lane outside the mission compound. Despite heavy rifle fire he was attempting to extinguish a blaze in one of the mission outbuildings. It was then that he was shot and fell to the ground. Then Miner saw his colleague, Dr. Chambers, run from the mission gate toward a body lying on the ground, and thinking that this was the body of a fellow misisonary, he helped Dr. Chambers carry the body back to the compound.

As they entered the gate, he wrote, "I looked down and for the first time saw the body that I was helping to carry. It was my own. And at that moment I felt free from my earthly body." He added that although his wife was in a city miles away at the time he was able to get to her side at once and impress upon her mind that he had survived physical death.

Some time later, after reading Miner Rogers' account of his own death, I met Dr. Chambers and told him of the message. He corroborated every detail I had already learned, but added one fascinating bit of information. "When I picked up Miner just after he was shot outside the compound," Dr. Chambers told me, "he was still breathing. He was alive. But as we entered the gate Miner gasped and died."

In other words, at the moment when Miner Rogers recognized his own body and knew that it was he who had been shot and who was being carried by Dr. Chambers—it was at that moment that he died.

Many persons who have been critically ill and who have been very near death have reported similar experiences of being detached from their physical bodies and being able to observe events outside the sickroom through some strange and unexplainable extension of their senses. A woman during a severe sickness found she could leave her physical body and could walk downstairs. She strolled through the rooms, somewhat confused but without pain, until she heard a voice commanding her to return to her physical body. She told me, "It took great effort to return, but I did."

And once when my sister Anna was extremely ill in a crowded hotel in Athens she "saw another country with a high wall and a gate, and I could see through the gate into a beautiful land, and I knew this was the other world. I wanted to go very much but I heard a voice say, 'Don't go. If you do you cannot return, and you are needed where you are.'" She, too, told me it was very difficult to resist the urge to pass through. And later when she was ill in a hospital she saw a beam of light leading up to a beautiful country, and she knew she could ascend to the peace and tranquility of the other world. But simultaneously she saw her husband kneeling beside his bed at home, praying for her, and again she resisted.

I have talked with half a dozen people who have had similar experiences. One case is most fascinating, involving a medical doctor with a strongly skeptical and practical turn of mind.

Critically ill and given up by his colleagues, the doctor was dying in his hospital bed. "Suddenly," he told me, "I found myself outside my physical body. I cannot explain it in any other words." He observed his nurse leaning against the wall of the room sobbing, and he watched attendants pull a sheet up over his physical body lying on the bed. He left the room then and strolled down the hall. He saw a wheeled stretcher pushed into Room 30 and return with a patient. He entered Room 31 and watched a nurse help a patient out of bed.

Then he heard a voice say, "You are not yet ready to come over. You must go back to your body." But he protested, for he did not want to go back. And the voice said, "But you must. Your work on earth is not yet finished." With great difficulty he got back into his physical body, and some time later regained consciousness.

His doctor and nurse were astonished. His colleague said, "By all tests you died, and now you are here again."

"Perhaps so," my friend replied weakly, "but I must know some things." He called the nurse and asked her to take careful notes on what he was to say. He told her what he had observed in the hall and in Room 31, and he asked her to check if these events had indeed happened as he had seen them. Naturally his nurse suspected delirium, for she knew he could not have observed what he had reported. She herself was unaware of what had happened outside the room, for she had remained there with her patient. But to humor him she granted his request and found that his report checked in every detail.

In comparison with the utopian words of our hymns and spirituals the descriptions of the world beyond are quite tame and unexciting. In most respects the people who have passed beyond are not much different mentally from the way they were here, and often they are doing the same kind of work and are concerned with the same things they were concerned with in this life.

But the reports indicate that there are no bars to the gates, that heaven is not an exclusive club for the religious elite, that there is no need for a passport issued by any particular religious sect here on earth. Roman Catholics are side by side with Unitarians and Moslems and pagans and Buddhists and atheists. The collected descriptions of this other world remind me of a joke a Unitarian friend recently told me.

It seems, my friend said, that a group of new arrivals were being taken on a guided tour of heaven by St. Peter. They passed a group of sour people, sitting quietly, obviously bored with themselves.

"Who are they?" asked one of the visitors.

"Oh, they're Episcopalians," St. Peter answered. "They're palled with heaven; they've done everything on earth."

Then they passed a high stone wall and they could hear voices from the other side.

"Who's in there?" a visitor asked.

St. Peter put his finger to his lips. "Shhhh. They're Roman Catholics. They don't think anyone else is here."

One message describing heaven came to us during a séance with the famous medium Arthur Ford. We had asked, "What is heaven like?"

And the answer was, "I am not in the kind of heaven you on earth think of. Over here are all kinds of people, many who did not know Christ on earth."

Such messages are not in accord with orthodox teachings and beliefs about salvation and immortality. In all the messages I have received and studied, some of them from former Roman Catholic priests, there is not the slightest evidence that either dogmatic belief or membership in orthodox churches is necessary to open the gates to God's heaven. Apparently we go over the border as persons—our personalities are unchanged; we go as selfish and as unselfish as we really are; we go as the noble or the evil characters that we are; and we go as the admixture of evil and noble, of good and bad, that we really are.

God's love includes us all; and He accepts us all, even the Hitlers and the Eichmanns and the Stalins and the Capones. But even His love cannot suddenly change a Hitler into an Albert Schweitzer. The love revealed in Jesus on the cross is a reconciling love which never admits defeat and which hopes to bring all His children back at last to the Father's home and family.

Heaven seems to be not a new life but an extension of life as we know it here; it seems to be a continuation of our lives here, except that there are no material things as we know them. The "things" of heaven are there, and they are the same as we know them here, but they are made material—if this word can be used in its earthly sense—only by the mind. It is the sort of thing that happens when a newly arrived spirit sees an older spirit in the form that the old-timer thinks the newcomer wishes to see. This is not materialization as we see it in séances and in demonstrations of what is called ectoplasm; it is the sort of materialization we all have experienced in dreams when we have seen our friends as they were ten years ago.

Again and again we receive messages such as this one recorded by a friend: "It is a good thing I was not looking for gold streets and wings! I have my work to do here, and when it is done I can visit with you on earth. The change from earth means that the horizon is broadened; it continues developing but is always vital and interesting. Someday you will learn that there is plenty of time. Live one day now; take tomorrow's troubles tomorrow."

Shortly after her death my sister Anna, communicating with us by Ouija board, told us of her activities in the other world. She was, she said, in charge of a home for children who had died as infants. With a staff of other young women as helpers she was teaching them and training them in a beautiful building surrounded by gardens. "I have every facility for helping these children gain in wisdom," she said. "Some of them are getting far better care and opportunity than they would have if they had remained longer on earth. Distraught parents need not grieve; their children are happy."

Another communication, not from Anna, said, "I have just attended a remarkable convocation here. We had a choir of what you call angels. I have never heard anything like it on earth. One of the speakers was St. Paul. What he said brought to mind what he had said in First Corinthians on immortality and love. There must have been at least five thousand persons in the great auditorium. Spiritual experiences of this kind are quite frequent over here, and are a great help to those seeking spiritual understanding but who were denied it on earth."

Of course such messages, especially this last one, seem utterly fantastic to us. Yet we are indeed simple-minded if on the one hand we believe in Christ and in St. Paul and in heaven and on the other hand say that St. Paul does not exist, that he is not in heaven, and that he would not be preaching there. Actually what would be more natural? What else would we expect St. Paul to be doing?

The composite picture of heaven, as gathered from hundreds of communications, describes it as having homes, libraries, concerts, and educational institutions of many sorts. Hosts of young people, either denied education on earth or desirous of continuing the process, are given opportunity to grow in knowledge and understanding. As in this world there are gardens, and beautiful color, and sounds, and fellowship.

We have reports of a young man whose great desire on earth was to play the violin but who could not because of poverty and environment. But there, in the other world, he is fulfilling his earthly wish and is studying under great teachers.

Another message, which I sincerely hope is accurate, said that no work of art is lost over there. In the libraries and museums and institutes are stored everything that has lifted man's spirits nearer God and flooded him with a sense of beauty and wonder. The great masterpieces of all time are there—Plato's *Phaedo*, St. Paul's Letter to the Corinthians, Bach's chorals, Handel's oratorios, Rembrandt's art, Rodin's sculpture. The result is, the message said, that countless multitudes who on earth were denied the joy of contemplating such beauty are given the fullest opportunity over there to appreciate these works of genius.

And we are told of great liberality there, both in little things, and in matters we consider very important here on earth. One of Marguerite Walter's communications about the World War I German army officer who had been killed while attempting to rescue one of his men included the information that for his first year on the other side he strutted around in his German uniform. The reports said that at this time he was still in a state of confusion, thinking he was still on the battlefield, and later he abandoned this dress. The comment was, "The less religious a person is on earth the more confused over here; the more religious the earth person is the easier the adjustment over here."

But this is minor liberality. Other reports indicate that married couples are not bound by legal, matrimonial, or sexual relationships that started here on earth. Relationships there are dependent on mutual spiritual understanding and harmony. Husbands and wives who shared such mutual love here continue to share it over there. But those who do not have spiritual experiences in common can go their own ways and are not required to live together. Couples whose spirits are utterly out of tune may part and find new companions, even though they were married on earth in St. Peter's or in the Mormon Temple in Salt Lake City. Surely this message seems in accordance with the loving spirit of Jesus.

In my files is the verbatim question-and-answer record of one session that should give much comfort to millions here on earth. It concerned a man named Everett who before his death had been blind from early childhood and in his later years was pitifully crippled with rheumatism in both hands and feet. This answer came in response to a question about him: "Everett is happy, filled with the beauty around him and not missing a jot. His hands are whole, his legs are whole, his eyes are whole; his heart will be whole when I tell him his son is listening. Over here we are full of joy for every chance to carry happy news. We all rejoice when one uses an established line of connection with loved ones."

Other interesting portions of that session follow:

"Miss Julia is here. She is a leader of her little group and is the same charming personality she was on earth. She says to you, 'Look up and smile for you have a world of happiness in your grasp. You need not look to far shores for beauty. You are surrounded by unselfish thoughts. Let love ease the load. So many are in want of love as they climb the hill of years.' "

Q. Is there punishment over there?

A. You would find it hard to inflict unnecessary pain. Do you think the love here is less than yours? Opportunity is given to rectify error.

Q. Are you helping others as you do us?

A. We try, but many eyes are blinded by material things. Others bar out help because of their selfishness, with minds open only to their own desires.

Q. How do you work with us here?

A. We cannot force ourselves on you, and we know only a bit more than you, although we have greater opportunities for growing in knowledge of the truth.

Q. Do you over there desire to communicate with us as much as we do with you?

A. More so. Many over here have been trying since man became a spirit, but seed must be planted in fertile soil to bring forth fruit.

Q.   We would like to know more about your life over there.

A.   You will have to wait until you come over yourselves. You still picture material objects. You cannot handle what we have. We have homes and communities, but you cannot handle our kitchen range. As long as you are bound by a physical body your mentality works in material terms. I have no physical body; the mind here is not confined.

Q.   Please tell us more about your life there.

A.   You want to skip some of the stairs. You must mount slowly and do each day's task to earn the fuller joy. What you accomplish now will not have to be done later.

Q.   How do people who have not known each other here come to know each other there.

A.   Likeness in mentality and spirituality draws people together here or there. The golden years are given for the tying of loose knots of our hurried years. Every wave has a trough as well as a crest. In progressing from crest to crest it is necessary to slide through the intervening trough. Slide easy and climb high. You are constantly questing for God. He is with you as much as He is with us, if you give Him a chance in your lives. Everett sends a message. He says, "I do not have to miss any of the beauty here, as I did in my blindness on earth. Beauty is all about us here. No one would dread to come if they could half guess what it is like. California will have to take a back seat; it is hard to describe."

Q.   When you speak of "here" what do you mean?

A.   Through the mists and into the sun, and you are here.

Q.   As the Bible says, "For He shall give His angels charge over thee." Is this the work you are doing?

A.   Yes, but we have no wings. Not even a halo.

Q.   It seems to us that many religious leaders try to hinder progress in this line.

A.   You are right. They ought to be beacon lights, but often they are bars to progress. This is not a new religion. Do not get the idea that it is something new. It is merely a demonstration to your minds, to those ready to receive it, of the age-old beauty in all true religion. All higher forms of religion teach immortality, but to some minds too close a connection between mortality and immortality terrifies them. Our demonstration needs no missionary work and should only pass from one receptive mind to others who are questing for truth and fuller knowledge.

Not long ago a skeptical friend, after reading the excerpts above, said, "Well, I guess I can accept it for what it is supposed to be, but if it is true that they have schools over there it might be wise if that particular spirit studied a little grammar and logic. This leaves more questions unanswered than before it started." Then after a pause he said thoughtfully, "But on the other hand I suppose they get only what we send them, and my grammar is far from perfect and the same with my logic."

Both Miner Rogers and Louise Andrews, both being well-educated persons on earth, were more articulate and complete in their communications. Both of them had been deeply consecrated to unselfish service for others, and, they reported, it was this type of work they were both doing on the other side.

Louise wrote of trying to help a girl who had been a prostitute on earth, and Louise was seeking to open her mind and heart to spiritual values. She wrote that one of the terrible things about a life of sensuality is that persons who have led such lives continued to seek to enter into the bodies of persons still on earth so that they can vicariously continue to have earthly sensations. She maintained that the vicious influence of a center of evil, of prejudice, of cruelty, of sensuality, of exploitation, was not only the result of earthly personalities but also the added influence of evil spirits with similar passions and desires. And when I read this message from her I was immediately reminded of my father's acceptance of the spirit world but his fundamental insistence that all communicating spirits were evil. Louise acknowledged the presence of Father's evil spirits, but she did not tell us that only the evil can communicate.

She also reported that countless spiritual personalities from the other side make their influence felt and strengthen the forces of good wherever prayer and service to God is the center of activities, such as at religious conferences.

And as I review these messages, filled with wonderment, astonishment, and confusion, considering myself a rational man, I turn to St. Paul for comfort. For he said, "Eye hath not seen, nor ear heard, neither have entered into the heart of man, the things which God hath prepared for them that love him. But God hath revealed them unto us by his Spirit; for the spirit searchest all things, yea, the deep things of God." (I Corinthians 2:9-10)

12

More than Mere Thoughts through Space

His voice in the darkness of the séance room in Philadelphia was deep and gruff and heavily accented, and he said he was Thunder Cloud, the spirit of an American Indian who had died some years previously.

I was there to witness the psychic power of Leonard Stott, a mild-mannered Philadelphia steamfitter with no advanced education but a simple and devout religious faith. It was Edward C. (Ned) Wood, a Quaker who has been my friend for more than forty years, who had brought me to meet L. S., as Stott was known among researchers in the paranormal. Also with us that night was Gilbert E. Wright, then a research chemist for General Electric in Schenectady.

L. S. had already gone into deep trance and through him came the independent voice of Thunder Cloud. He spoke for a while, his heavy voice impressive but saying little of importance that night, and then he was gone. There was silence for a while and we could hear only L. S. breathing softly in the darkness. Then we heard a young girl's voice, and Ned Wood whispered to me, "It's Barbara. Barbara Hutchinson. She comes almost as often as the Indian."

It was not the conversation or the messages that were important that evening; it was the apport that Barbara performed. As calmly as if such an extraordinary event were commonplace, and indeed it seemed to be at the Stott's house, Barbara said, "I will bring you a fresh rose from a distant garden." Within a few minutes we heard something drop lightly on the table in front of us, and when we turned on the light there lay a beautiful, freshly cut red rose, its petals still damp with dew.

I visited Leonard Stott three times, and each time some object was apported, brought into the closed room, supposedly by spirits using paranormal techniques. Of course I had experienced apports previously, and had studied them ever since my mother had showed me the underlined forty-nine-word message apported by my sister Anna two weeks after her death. And therefore I was not too surprised by these almost routine demonstrations by the spirits who came to us through L. S.

But one apport, experienced there by Gilbert Wright, was indeed remarkable. It was brought by Thunder Cloud, and in the words of Gilbert Wright, who corresponded extensively with me about the experience, it was "placed in my hands without feeling or fumbling as though the donor could see in the dark." It appeared to be "a clod of hard earth, half clay and half sand, with a sprig of wild asparagus growing out of one corner and a sprig of clover out of the other. Both were fresh!"

The clod weighed slightly more than four pounds, and when Wright returned to his home after the sitting he examined it more closely. The soil (four ounces of it, according to Wright's meticulous records) was so thick that Wright did not suspect that it might be concealing other objects. Carefully he began to pare the soil away from the lump and found 1) a large stone ax weighing two pounds, 2) a stone maul weighing fourteen ounces, 3) a large arrowhead, and 4) a small arrowhead.

"I spent half an hour," he wrote me, "scraping off the dirt which adhered very tightly. I had literally to dig the dirt from the grooves in the stone implements before they became visible." He carefully preserved the soil for later analysis and submitted the stone artifacts to an Indian expert for identification. The expert reported: "The stone implements are of argillite, a mineral resembling basalt. They were used by the Coastal Algonkins about 1000 A.D. The maul is a particularly good specimen. Few museums could boast a better. . . . The soil came from Camden, N.J., or somewhere in the vicinity of Philadelphia. It is called a micaceous steatite. A bed of it stretches up the Susquehanna Valley to Lancaster, Pa."

Later an amateur anthropologist and collector offered to buy the ax and maul for fifty dollars. Arguing with himself, Wright wrote me, "Now assuming these implements to have been fraudulently introduced into the séance room, where did the Stotts get them? Had they been stolen from a museum, they would have been clean. They could not have been purchased from a pawn shop for the same reason. The only relevant theory that is left, if we take the oblique view, is that the Stotts have found a deposit somewhere, probably in their own back yard. But how did they recognize the find in the first place? In the condition in which they were received [by Wright] they were not recognizably artifacts. I couldn't have recognized them and I am scientifically trained, and, I believe, more observant than the Stotts.

"Besides, I cannot see how they could have been brought secretly into the séance room. There was nothing of that sort in the room when we entered. The sprig of asparagus might have been pinned up behind the curtain and likewise the clump of clover, but the floor was of linoleum and there was no sand on it. If fraudulently introduced, they must have been concealed in a bag and that would have been too bulky a parcel to conceal about one's person. Lastly they are worth about fifty dollars for they are all excellent speciments. So, on the oblique theory, the Stotts accept a dollar fee [for the séance] and hand out goods to the value of fifty dollars. That doesn't make sense!"

And later Wright wrote me about other apports he had received. "Under strict test conditions I have received an ancient coin, an issue of India and approximately two thousand years old. I have received two absolutely fresh poppies when none were available at that time of year in that particular zone. I have received an English farthing, an Egyptian curio—presumably from Cario—ten artificial gems, a small seashell, a child's sleigh bell; and I have had the phenomenon of apportion take place in my own apartment in broad daylight, a package of cigarettes vanishing from a closed desk and dropping in the middle of the floor in front of us, a small bell being torn from a curtain where it was sewn and placed on the middle of a studio couch, and many other phenomena."

A friend recently remarked to me that this would indeed be a fascinating and inexpensive way of collecting a small, private museum. And this would be true if the *method* of acquisition was obviously not more important than the acquisition itself. For we cannot explain the apport, although we know it exists. Some apports, of course, are the result of shameless and deliberate trickery, and these we can dismiss. But what of those that so far defy explanation? Can we believe that they are what they purport to be? Are they really the use of physical principles that even our best scientists have not yet discovered? And more important, are they actually performed by spirits or "angels" or personalities who have survived the experience of death? For if they are, then we do have proof of immortality.

It was an apport that was the clinching bit of evidence for my good friend Dr. Sherwood Eddy. Despite years of research and experience, including experience with apports for other persons, he waited several years for his own apport before writing his excellent and convincing book, *You Will Survive After Death*.

Sherwood Eddy and I have know each other for more than fifty years. Together we have journeyed on land and sea throughout the world, and always we have shared our deepest thoughts and problems. I have much to thank him for, but I am most grateful to him for introducing me to Dr. E. A. Macbeth, a New York medium, and to Father Tobe, Dr. Macbeth's spirit control.

Dr. Macbeth, a former practicing physician who had turned to business interests, had exceptional psychic gifts. His abilities included independent writing, in which no human hand touches the pencil or paper; the use of direct voice, in which spirits speak with their own voices and not through the lips of a medium; and for forty years he had been in regular contact with Father Tobe, a former Roman Catholic priest. Tobe, as he simply signed his written messages to us, had been born in Ireland and came to America in his early days in the priesthood. He gave the date of his death as April 2, 1852, and he is buried in Elizabethtown, Kentucky.

I joined Sherwood Eddy in several sittings at Dr. Macbeth's New York City apartment and found Father Tobe a most interesting, intelligent personality. He was warm, friendly, humorous, and understanding. Our chats with him—while Dr. Macbeth sat quietly in his armchair, listening to the conversation—were sometimes on theology, sometimes involved with the introduction of others who had passed over, and were always rewarding. But my most interesting experience in the Macbeth household was Father Tobe's demonstration of independent writing.

The room was fully lighted and I was able to observe all that took place. A small pad of paper was placed on the table in front of us and we all placed our hands on it for a few moments. Then each of us examined the pad carefully, turning the leaves to be sure that nothing was already written on it.

The pad was then placed in the center of the table with a small pencil beside it, and a green cloth was dropped over it. With three others I held this cloth lightly above the pad so that its edges draped down onto the table top and made a sort of lightproof tent for the writing materials. All the hands of those present were always in sight.

Soon I heard distinct taps on the pad, and Father Tobe's rich deep voice announced that he would then write on the pad. I distinctly felt vibrations under the cloth and could hear the pencil scratching on the pad. The writing continued for several minutes, and when it stopped Father Tobe gave three distinct taps with the pencil on the pad.

When we lifted the cloth and took up the pad we found several pages covered with fine writing in pencil. Father Tobe's message was concerned with the troubled conditions in the world, and he urged us all to devote our lives to working for peace. He also gave some personal and intimate messages to Sherwood Eddy and his wife from their daughter in the other world.

It was some time after this that Sherwood told me of the personal apport that Father Tobe had performed for him. Sherwood had witnessed several of Father Tobe's apports over the years and had been impressed by and intrigued with them. In one case Tobe had transported, in a matter of seconds, a tiny porcelain figurine across Manhattan, and later he had brought a heavy wrought-iron ash tray from Chicago to New York City while the Macbeth group was singing the first stanza of "Nearer My God to Thee."

But Sherwood felt he must have a personal experience, involving some of his personal property, before he had enough convincing evidence to write the book he had planned and had talked over with Father Tobe.

And one night when the Eddys were at Dr. Macbeth's home in Rhinebeck-on-Hudson, a hundred miles from the Eddys' Jackson Heights, Long Island, apartment, Father Tobe agreed. He described the Eddy apartment in minute detail, even including some photographs on the mantel. Then he asked Sherwood if he had a pair of enameled ash trays in the apartment. When Sherwood admitted that he had, Father Tobe said that he would bring one to the Macbeth home.

After approximately fifteen minutes, one of the trays dropped out of the air and struck Sherwood's hand. He told me that he then marked it with a cross, for identification, and that night when he returned to his apartment he found one ash tray missing, although its mate was in the usual place. The ash tray he had received from Father Tobe was the one missing from his apartment.

In the mass of psychic phenomena, apports are comparatively rare, and the few authentic cases that exist have yet to yield information of a higher meaning. Perhaps there is some merit to the viewpoint of Gilbert Wright when he writes me:

"I am coming to the conclusion that the task of psychic research is futile. The higher can never be expressed in terms of the lower. We cannot understand clairvoyance until we become clairvoyant ourselves; then no explanation is necessary. Science, reasoning, intelligence are but tools that we use to compensate for our lack of 'sight' or 'insight.' Science has to arrive at her conclusions the hard way. In the words of Claude Bragdon: 'The consummation devoutly to be desired is not the pushing to the limits of the possible in the physical world, but the expansion of consciousness itself.' "

13

The Shanti Devi Case

When the girl was four years old she told her amused parents that her name was really Ludgi, and not Shanti Devi as she had been named. And a few years later she began to describe, in some detail, a village named Muttra where she said she had once lived, yet her parents knew that she had never been away from the tiny settlement in India where she had been born.

By her eleventh birthday the tale had grown to involve a previous life in which she had been married to a Muttra man named Kedar Nath Chaubey. As his wife, she said, she had given birth to three children, and it was during the birth of the third, a daughter, that she had died. The specific details of this other life grew as little Shanti told her stories, and the tale spread throughout India.

In the Western world her accounts would have been regarded as youthful fantasy; reincarnation, for some reason, seems absurd and even repugnant to many of us. But in India, where millions regard pre-existence with as much respect as we regard Christianity, there was excitement in many circles. It was as if an American child had discovered the exact spot where Leif Ericson landed in America a thousand years ago, for although we know that Leif discovered America we do not know what spot he trod.

At the Univeristy of Bombay a research committee was formed to investigate the case. In addition to university professors the committee included a lawyer and a publisher, and these men, trained in the recognition of acts, visited little Shanti Devi. She not only repeated her story, insisting on its truth, but she expanded it. She told the investigators the names of the three children she had borne in an earlier life; she described the color of their hair and eyes; she named the members of her husband's family; she described the streets and the buildings of Muttra.

Then the committee decided to test the little girl who so insistently said she had been someone else in another life. They took her by train from the native village that she had never left in her life, to Muttra—which she had never seen. There her head was wrapped with a scarf so that she could not see, for she had said she knew Muttra so well that she need not see it. And she led the committee down the streets of the village, describing accurately what she could not see, and describing what was yet to come around the next unturned turning. She guided them without hesitation, and when they reached a narrow lane she told them that this was where she once lived.

When the blindfold was unfastened she saw an old man sitting outside the house. She greeted him in the dialect of Muttra, although she had spoken only Hindustani until that moment, and she told investigators, "He is the grandfather of Ludgi, the woman I once was before I died in this house giving birth to a daughter." The old man gave no sign of recognition to the strange girl, but he was indeed the grandfather of Ludgi. Inside the house were gathered the relatives and neighbors of the dead Ludgi, waiting to meet Shanti Devi, and the little eleven-year-old girl passed from one to another of them, calling each one of them, correctly, by name.

When she saw her "former husband," Kedar Nath Chaubey, she greeted him by name, and reminded him of a dozen intimate details of his life with Ludgi, and the astonished man stood and nodded in amazed agreement. Shanti told him that when she had been Ludgi and his wife she had hidden some coins in the corner of an underground room, but that when she returned for them they had disappeared. And the embarrassed man admitted that he himself had found the coins and taken them.

This was the story of Shanti Devi as I had read it in 1938 in *The New York Times* and news magazines shortly before Marion and I boarded a ship for a world lecture tour under the auspices of the Carnegie Endowment for International Peace. It fascinated us, of course, but neither of us had any intimation that in India we were to come on further evidence of this mysterious case.

A few months later we spent a week at Isabella Thoburn College in Lucknow, India, where we both gave a series of talks. Isabella Thoburn is a Methodist college for women, and we frequently took our meals with the students. One evening at dinner with a group of seniors—some Hindu, some Moslem, some Christian—I recounted the story of Shanti Devi and then asked the young women if any of them had heard the story. Directly opposite me sat a bright young senior, a leader of her class, a particularly attractive and intelligent girl who had been exceptionally attentive to my words about Shanti Devi. When I had finished she pulled her sari higher on her shoulder, as if she were delaying her decision, and then she spoke.

"Dr. Harlow," she said quietly in her excellent English, "this is most interesting. I come from Muttra; my home is there; my parents live there. And the house where Ludgi died is just across the street from my house. My mother was Ludgi's closest friend and had known her since they were little children."

She paused then, her eyes half closed in thought. "You should know that my family has been Christian for two generations; we do not believe in reincarnation as the Hindus do. But I will tell you this in all truth. When Shanti Devi was brought to Muttra my mother was asked to be one of the group to meet her in the house of Kedar Nath Chaubey. When my mother was a little girl and played with Ludgi they had secret names for each other, as little girls do. They called each other by these names, and they were the only ones who knew these names. When this eleven-year-old girl, Shanti Devi, came face to face with my mother she clasped her hands and called her by that secret name."

She looked at me and at the other girls at the table. "This is what my mother told me. We do not explain it. We do not believe in reincarnation, but we were all mystified by this experience. Have you any explanation?"

I shook my head. No, I did not have an adequate explanation then, and I do not now. I have never heard what became of Shanti Devi, and I do not know the result of the professional committee's investigation. But the intriguing question of reincarnation is still with us, as it has been since before Christ.

Many scholars have pointed out that if we consider the soul immortal, it is just as logical to give it an infinite *past* as to give it an infinite *future*. They ask, in other words: Does the act of birth as we know it actually *manufacture* the soul, or did the soul already exist and merely occupy the manufactured body? Can there not also be a herebefore as well as a hereafter?

Now reincarnation is not to be confused with the Hindu belief in transmigration. This belief holds that the soul at death may pass into the body of another person or of an animal; reincarnation affirms only the possibility of being born again into another human body. Reincarnation is a belief that we are but temporary expressions of the immortal soul, which is the *real person*.

Those who believe this theory maintain that having been incarnated once, as we were at birth, we may well have been incarnated in other bodies in times past. When we read classical literature or the Bible we discover that this idea has gripped the minds of men for generations. In both Hinduism and Buddhism it plays an important role, but we also find it in Greek and Roman literature. Plato and Pythagoras mention it, and even some of the early Christian writers mention it. As a matter of fact it was not until the Council of Constantinople in the year 553 that the Christian church denounced reincarnation as heresy.

Ceasar writes that the Druids of Gaul held this belief, and in later times such men as Giordano Bruno, Swedenborg, Goethe, Hume, and Schopenhauer advocated this theory. Dean W. R. Inge goes so far as to assert, "I find the doctrine both credible and attractive."

We find references to reincarnation in many of our more modern writers and poets, including Browning, Longfellow, and Wordsworth. In his book *The Imprisoned Splendor* Raynor Johnston reminds us that the poet John Masefield once wrote:

> I hold that when a person died
>   His soul returns again to earth;
> Arrayed in some new flesh-disguise,
>   Another mother gives him birth.
> With sturdier limbs and brighter brain
>   The old soul takes the road again.

We would be quite shortsighted if we dismissed this theory as the belief of only primitive and illiterate minds. Actually reincarnation is as good an explanation for the "I've been here before" experience as are dreams, and in some cases a much more logical explanation.

And to look at the problem as through the back of a mirror, we can find some parallel between the blanked-out memories of our first few years of life and the problem of why we do not remember our previous incarnations if we are indeed reincarnated. For example only yesterday I was looking at a photograph taken when I was two years old. In the picture are my father and mother and sister. My father has his arm around me. At that time, when I was two years old, I knew these people and called them by name. I knew the house where we lived; I knew the room where I slept; I knew and walked the streets outside.

Yet I have no memory of this. I cannot recall a single incident of having lived in Brooklyn, yet I did so for two years. I cannot recall that particular image of my parents or sister; only the photographic image remains to remind me that I am the same spirit that dwelt in that little boy of two having his picture taken. In reincarnation, its advocates would point out, there is no picture to point out how our memories have failed.

Many problems would be solved if reincarnation is a fact. And one of them is the explanation of child prodigies and geniuses. How can you explain Mozart, the believers of reincarnation ask, unless he was given a running start in some earlier life? Can you really say, they ask, that when a four-year-old plays the clavichord and composes minuets this is merely accelerated development of an otherwise normal child? And Mozart's youthful history, like that of other prodigies and geniuses, is indeed tantalizing from this viewpoint. At six he played before the Emperor Francis I; at seven he was writing symphonies and had published six sonatas; when he was thirteen the prince archbishop of Salzburg named his director of concerts, and he composed the opera *Mitridate*.

The reincarnationists, listing the prodigies in mathematics, chemistry, art, and literature, ask: Whence came this knowledge? For them, there is only one answer, and it explains such minds as Bacon, Shakespeare, and Einstein. The answer, they say, lies in the accumulated wisdom from past incarnations.

There are, however, strong opponents of this theory. At Columbia University Dr. James Hyslop, a scientific researcher into psychical phenomena, attacks the theory as "containing nothing desirable and nothing ethical." He writes, "The absolutely fundamental condition of all ethics is memory and the retention of personal identity, and the memory and personal identity are excluded from the processes of reincarnation."

Even so we find passages in the New Testament which seem to indicate that belief in reincarnation was prevalent among the Jews of Jesus' time. When Jesus asks his disciples (Matthew 16:13-14; Mark 8:27-28; and Luke 9:18-19), "Whom do men say that I am?" they reply, "Some say John the Baptist; some Elijah; and others Jeremiah, or one of the prophets." In Matthew 11:14, when Jesus discusses the common belief that before the Messiah came Elijah the prophet would return as a forerunner, he says to the crowd around him, "If ye are willing to accept it, he is Elija who is to come," referring to John the Baptist. Spiritualists maintain that this affirms that John the Baptist was the spirit of Elijah reincarnated.

Reincarnation, according to its adherents, gives God an opportunity to make up for the frustrations, the injustices, and the brevity of many lives. In another incarnation such spirits will be given the opportunities denied them in their previous earth lives and justice will triumph over wrong.

I do not see, in the light of the evidence we now have, that the case for reincarnation can be proved or disproved. I cannot accept the reincarnationists' explanation of prodigies; I do not know how to explain

Shanti Devi; and I am unable to agree with Dr. Hyslop's argument that loss of memory vitiates Christian ethics.

But I am willing, even eager, to hear more about this fascinating subject. For it opens up new realms of thought, realms that are more important than subpolar exploration, more important than space rocketry, more important than pounds of thrust and apogees and perigees. These are the realms that can answer whence we came and where we go, and it is these questions that confound our souls.

14

We Question a "Talking" Horse

In retrospect I suppose I seemed ridiculous standing there in a Richmond, Virginia, stable, looking at the broad white stripe on the forehead of a docile, sleepy brown mare named Lady Wonder, and asking her questions.

But on the other hand I was no more ridiculous than the Massachusetts district attorney who later asked the same horse to help him find a four-year-old boy who had vanished two years earlier. For we both got answers, and they were accurate.

To the district attorney the mare replied, "Pittsfield Water Wheel," which meant nothing to the official. But when a police officer suggested that the message may have been a garbled version of "Field and Wilde Water Pit," an abandoned quarry in the area, the mare's psychic ability was further proved. The boy's body was found there.

My visit to the "talking" horse was as satisfactory and as mystifying as the district attorney's. We got results, but neither of us can explain them.

In 1957, when Lady Wonder died of a heart attack at the age of thirty-three, she had been investigated by a score of researchers including Dr. Rhine, who had made a special trip from Duke University to spend several days with her. Rhine reported her telepathic; others asserted that Lady Wonder was merely a trick horse; some said she was an animal medium being controlled by an intelligence from the spirit world, much as Margery was controlled by Walter.

Whatever Lady Wonder actually was she was remarkable. Her obituary pointed out that after the body of little Danny Matson was found in the quarry, thousands of letters, telegrams, and telephone calls besieged her owner and master, Mrs. Claudia Fonda. A Texan asked for tips on where to drill for oil; hundreds of Americans, probably hoping to make the phrase "right from the horse's mouth" a literal one, wanted Lady Wonder to pick the winners at race tracks.

During her inordinately long life Lady correctly predicted the winner (Dempsey) of the Dempsey-Sharkey fight in 1927 when she was only three years old; she foretold the sex of unborn infants; she could identify the maiden names of her callers; once she told me, accurately, that my granddaughter Linda was living in Athens.

Lady Wonder answered her questions on a horse-sized typewriter especially designed for her. When asked a question aloud she would peck out the answer by nudging the keyboard with her nose. She was twenty-four years old and had been operating her typewriter for some years when I made the first of several visits to Richmond to see her. We paid our small fee to Mrs. Fonda, for the horse was on public exhibition, and were led into the stable where Lady, a gentle, quiet animal seemed almost bored with us. She stood in front of her typewriter, and Mrs. Fonda stood about six feet away from us.

Mrs. Fonda said, "Ask any question you like, but please concentrate on the answer." I nodded and we started.

Taking a blank card and a pencil from my pocket I began to scribble. I wrote circles and x's and lines, keeping the pencil moving, and while doing so I wrote the only intelligible symbol on the pad, the figure 8.

"Lady," I asked, "will you add 2 to the figure I have written?"

With no hesitation the horse nosed up the figure 10. I then wrote the figure 20 and said nothing. Lady nosed up the number.

Then I wrote the numeral 4. "Divide the number I have written by two," I said. Without a pause she nosed up 2. Marion took her turn with the horse, giving her simple arithmetical problems such as a child of ten might be able to solve—addition, division, subtraction, and multiplication. And Lady answered accurately and quickly.

"What is the name of our oldest granddaughter?" I asked. Mrs. Fonda had no way of knowing the answer to this, of course, and Marion and I were particularly careful to avert our eyes, so that in case the horse were trained to nudge the letters we looked at, we would not be helping her. If she were going to get the answers, we felt, she would have to do it by telepathy and not with the techniques of professional magic. She made two false starts on this question, and each time I said, "No, Lady." On the third attempt she correctly nosed up the word "Linda."

Marion asked, "What is my husband's first name?" Lady spelled out "Ralph." "What is our son's name?" Lady answered correctly, "John."

For almost an hour we questioned the horse, and although there were several false starts, always Lady answered correctly. As the session went on she seemed to grow tired and the answers came more slowly.

Some time later a friend of mine, a professor at Amherst College and a decided skeptic about extrasensory perception, visited Lady after we had told him about our experience. When he returned he was no longer scoffing at Lady's performances. As she had for us, Lady solved several mathematical problems for our friend and also correctly spelled out his son's name—an uncommon one—then told him the name of the street on which he lived. But his previous position on ESP, that there is no such thing, was unchanged. He told me, "I still think there is some trick back of it."

Of course it is possible that he is right. But if so it was truly remarkable legerdemain. Throughout our visits Mrs. Fonda stood behind the horse. It was impossible for her to see what I wrote on my card; it was equally impossible for her to know the answers to the questions we asked. Both Marion and I were extremely careful not to look at upcoming letters on the keyboard. Only we knew the answers, yet Lady Wonder "typed" them out for us.

Before our first visit a professor of psychology told us that it was impossible for a horse to give a correct answer to a question unless the person in charge of the horse knew both the question and the answer. But the impossible had happened: Lady Wonder had answered us.

One explanation, almost as weird as the experience itself, is that Mrs. Fonda received the answers from us by telepathy and then transmitted them by telepathy to the horse. But telepathy from Mrs. Fonda to the horse is no less remarkable than telepathy from me to the horse. When I pointed this out during one discussion the skeptic said, "Well, then Mrs. Fonda secretly signals the answer to the horse. It's a trick. Blamed clever, but still a trick." If we assume this to be the case how do we explain the horse's ability to transfer a secret signal from its master into an intelligible combination of the twenty-six letters in the English alphabet? Certainly the answer is much simpler and more understandable than this, or wondrously more complicated.

When Mrs. Fonda bought Lady in 1925 the filly was two weeks old—an ordinary horse in ordinary surroundings. Mrs. Fonda was not then, and is not now, interested in ESP or paranormal phenomena. In fact I was rather perplexed during our first visit when I discovered that she had no knowledge of such psychical terms as ectoplasm, apport, or levitation. She was simply interested in horses, certainly not in psychic mysteries.

But one day Mrs. Fonda noticed that the colt seemed to sense when Mrs. Fonda wanted her in the barn. Whenever she went out to call Lady from the field, the horse was already on her way. This would not have been unusual if the horse had seen Mrs. Fonda and simply associated her with food or water or affection. But that was not the case. The horse was coming to the barn before Mrs. Fonda could be seen; she was coming when Mrs. Fonda *wanted* her to come. Mrs. Fonda then tested the horse. She would hide, certain that Lady had not seen her, and then *will* her to come. Lady responded, and Mrs. Fonda wondered what she had in her barn. As the horse grew older Mrs. Fonda tested her more and more until she reached the point where the typewriter was built for her.

As remarkable as was Lady Wonder, the famous Eberfeld horses of West Prussia were even more astounding. There were four of them: Muhamed and Zarif, Arabian stallions; Kluge Hans, a Russian stallion; and Hanschen, a Shetland pony. The intellectual abilities of these animals stirred up an academic whirlpool that frothed in Europe for years. It started shortly before World War I when a retired schoolteacher named Von Osten began to experiment with Kluge Hans. He was convinced that some animals could reason and that they could be taught far beyond the peaks exhibited by circus animals.

When he announced that his stallion had been trained to the level of a fourteen-year-old boy, investigators began to arrive. They found that the horse could read some words; he could tell time, knew the days of the week, and could solve mathematical problems. When Von Osten died the horse was inherited by Karl Krall, a wealthy industrialist who had been intrigued by Von Osten's work. Krall added the three other horses to his intellectual stable and continued the training. Soon the Arabians had surged past Kluge Hans, with Muhamed far ahead. Quickly he learned to read and spell, communicating by tapping out the numerical position of letters marked on a chart. In mathematics he could extract square, cube, and fourth roots; once an investigator asked him for the fourth root of 7,890,481 and Muhamed tapped our the correct answer—53—within a matter of seconds.

The famous Belgian philosopher Maurice Maeterlinck, a 1911 Nobel Prize winner, was one of the Eberfeld investigators. He was startled by his visit and wrote, "I have testified with the same scrupulous accuracy as though I were reporting a criminal trial in which a man's life depended upon that accuracy." Left alone in the stable with Muhamed, he decided to test the horse's spelling ability and "spoke the first word that came into my head—'Weidenhof,' the name of my hotel. Muhamed at once rapped back 'Weidenhoz' and I wrote each letter as it came through. I felt the breath of the abyss on my face. I could not have been more astonished if I had heard a voice from the dead." When the owner saw the error a few minutes later he said, "Muhamed, correct your mistake," and the horse at once tapped out the letter f.

Only recently Dr. William Mackenzie, who taught for years at Genoa University in Italy, reviewed his investigation of the horses in 1913. He reported that he was sure there had been no trickery, telepathy, or secret signals. He pointed out that the animals had actually conversed with the investigators, rapping out spontaneous answers, and in addition had mentally solved mathematical problems that humans could approach only with paper and pencil. He suggested that the horses were mediums.

The four animals died during the war after more than 150 scholarly articles were written about their abilities. But no scholar advanced a universally accepted explanation. Like the more recent and less intellectual Lady Wonder, the Eberfeld horses are riddles of the mind—so far unexplained yet tantalizing with their hints of new, exciting, important knowledge still to be discovered.

15

Kivie and I Visit Arthur Ford

Kivie Kaplan is one of the kindest men I know, a sort of paragon of philanthropy mixed with a paradoxically no-nonsense business acumen that has made him an extremely successful Boston businessman. Marion and I have known Kivie and his wife, Emily, for many, many years; we have been the recipients of their hospitality and their generosity; we have heard Kivie's intelligent but kind laughter when we have not been too objective in describing paranormal phenomena.

Therefore it was with some sense of curiosity when in January of 1957, while we were all in New York City, I asked the Kaplans to join me at a sitting with the Reverend Arthur Ford, one of the most famous and respected of the world's psychic mediums. "Kivie," I said, "I am convinced that there is no living person in this country today who has such psychic gifts as Arthur Ford. I called on him once before five years ago. He's remarkable. Would you and Emily like to come with me this time?"

Kivie said yes, it might be fun, and I immediately telephoned Arthur Ford from my hotel room, asking for an appointment for the three of us. As we were leaving, Mrs. Lou Shapiro, the wife of a New York diagnostician and a long-time mutual friend, dropped by to see us. Like the Kaplans, Sue Shapiro had never attended a séance, and I urged her to join us. She shrugged agreement, and we were on our way, without Arthur Ford's knowing she was coming.

Arthur Ford, as I explained to my guests as we drove to his hotel, is perhaps best known to the general public for his aid in deciphering the famous Houdini code by which the magician communicated with his wife after his death. Another famous magician, Howard Thurston, who had once bitterly attacked psychic mediums as frauds, later publicly recanted to Ford, telling the audience that Ford was "a man whom I firmly believe can help you to communicate with your beloved dead."

In the last forty years Ford has traveled around the world many times, lecturing and demonstrating his remarkable abilities. Queen Maud of Norway once asked for a private sitting and later presented him with a British Royal Signet, containing seventy-three small diamonds. His public appearances have attracted huge audiences, and, for example, in Brisbane, Australia, he spoke to more than three thousand six hundred persons in the Town Hall.

Ford's first contact with psychic experience came when he was a young second lieutenant stationed at Camp Grant during World War I. Previously he had been a theology student but had interrupted his college training to volunteer for the Army. One night in 1917, at the height of the influenza epidemic, young Lt. Ford dreamed he saw a roster of dead men's names. He was not too surprised at this because one of his daily duties was to post the list of influenza victims on a camp bulletin board. However, the next day, when he picked up the sheet from the adjutant's office he was startled to find that the list was identical, even in sequence, with the roster he had seen in his dream.

With something less than amusement he told his tent mate of the dream, and the friend scoffed. But the following morning, after he had again dreamed that day's list even before it had been reported to the adjutant, he wrote down the names of the dead while his friend watched. When the list was posted it was identical with Ford's list. Not much later, in his dreams, he began to receive combat casualty lists several days before the newspapers published them.

After the war he returned to his ministerial training and was ordained. But his wartime experiences had awakened in him a strong interest in the paranormal. He continued to read and investigate, and his abilities became more sensitive. In 1924, while he was in a slight trance, he was visited by an invisible personality who introduced himself as Fletcher, a boyhood friend who had been killed in the war. Ford could not remember Fletcher, and at the spirit's second visit a friend of Ford's questioned him. Fletcher replied that he was using his middle name because his family was Roman Catholic and he did not wish to cause them discomfort simply because Fletcher had found conditions in the other world somewhat different from what his family believed them to be.

The spirit said that he had moved from Fort Pierce, Florida, where both he and Ford had lived, when he was about nine years old. And he gave specific information regarding his death in combat; he named his company and regiment, and he gave the address of his family, who were then living in Canada. Extremely curious, Ford wrote the family, giving no information on his part, but asking, among other questions about the family, for some news of Fletcher. The reply confirmed the information that Ford had received in trance, even corroborating the time and place of Fletcher's death as well as his regimental identification.

Since that time Fletcher has been Ford's "control," acting much as did Walter for his sister Margery. The partnership has been consistent and continuous since 1924, and when the Kaplans and Mrs. Shapiro and I went calling that afternoon we really were going to hear Fletcher bring us messages through the mediumship of Arthur Ford.

As I introduced my guests to Ford I saw that he was unchanged since I last had seen him. I was again impressed by his utter simplicity, humility, and sincerity. A heavy man of average height and with a high forehead, he is calm, gentle, quiet, and not given to small talk. After introductions he looked squarely at Emily Kaplan and told her that she had psychic powers—"I see an aura around your head." And then he went to work. He stretched out on a sofa and dropped a black scarf over his eyes. Within seconds he appeared to be in a deep, restful sleep but actually he was in trance. We were quiet, waiting, for several minutes and then Fletcher began to speak, bringing us messages for an hour and a half.

A visit with Ford—or more properly with Fletcher—can best be described as a Christmas Day long-distance telephone call with a dozen members of a family all clamoring around the instrument, instructing the speaker to ask this question and that, sending messages that are often incomplete if not incoherent, interrupting, forgetting important matters, but delighted at the contact across the miles of space.

At this moment I am reading the typescript of the notes I made during the ninety-minute séance, and it seems to me that the best way to capture the spirit, the feeling, and the accuracy of an experience with Fletcher is to insert part of the verbatim record. It follows:

> *Fletcher:* Hello, I have met you before. [He was speaking to me.]
> *Harlow:* Hello, Fletcher. This is Mr. and Mrs. Kaplan and Mrs. Shapiro.
> *Fletcher:* I am glad to meet you all. Over here we make a distinction between religion and spirituality. Many people who are formally

religious are not spiritual, and many who do not seem connected with formal religion are deeply spiritual. Race is not geographical and religion is universal. [This comment greatly interested me because here was Fletcher, a former Roman Catholic, speaking to three Jews. Then suddenly, as if he had finished a required, formal introduction, he changed the subject.]

Fletcher: There are several people who want to speak with you. A man tells me his name is Herman and that he is well and happy over here.

Emily Kaplan: I had a brother Herman. He died several years ago. [At this point Fletcher gave Emily several intimate and personal messages that I do not wish to reveal. These gave evidence that the message was indeed from her brother, and Emily was deeply moved.]

Fletcher: Kivie's mother is here. You look like your mother, Kivie. She wishes me to say that in her last years on earth you did all you could for her and she is most grateful. She has no conscious memory of when or how she passed away. She says that had she lived longer in your world she would have been an increasing burden, so she is glad she escaped from it for her sake and for yours.

[Both Marion and I had known Kivie's mother well, and the messages, many of which I do not include because they are personal and intimate, gave evidence of coming from the same sort of person we had known. Kivie's devotion to his mother had been most admirable. Every morning on his way to his office he would drop in to see her. She had become very helpless, both physically and mentally, toward the close of her life, and Kivie gave unselfishly to her needs. Both Marion and I were witnesses to his wonderful care for her. As Fletcher relayed Mrs. Kaplan's messages, Kivie grew excited with delight. It was his first experience with psychic messages, and the remarks he was receiving were both humorous and very much the type his mother was wont to make.]

Fletcher (suddenly changing the subject): Mrs. Shapiro, do you at times wear a white uniform? Do you work in a hospital?

Mrs. Shapiro: I often wear a white uniform when working in my husband's clinic, but I have not worked in a hospital for years.

Fletcher: Mrs. Kaplan wants me to say this: Kivie and Emily, I did not wholly approve of your marriage. I thought you were too young at that time but I changed my mind. Emily, you have been a good wife to Kivie and you have been so happy together that I came to approve wholly. I am grateful for all you have been doing to help refugees and others in need. Do not be alarmed about Israel. It is going to work out well. I am glad you are not too deeply involved in this trouble. You and Emily have been in the Near East recently so you know about this problem. [The Kaplans had visited Israel the previous spring.]

Fletcher: Dr. Harlow, there is a lady here who says her name is Myra and wants to give you a greeting.

Harlow: What is the lady's last name?

Fletcher: She says it is Wilson. [Immediately I remembered Myra Wilson, a member of my department at Smith for several years who had died of cancer three years previously. I had recommended her for the position of headmistress of the Northfield School for Girls, and she had become one of the school's great leaders.]

Fletcher: Myra asks why Moody founded Northfield.

Harlow: She knows the answer better than anyone.

Fletcher: Myra sends regards to Virginia at Smith. [Virginia Corwin is now chairman of the department of religion at Smith.]

Fletcher (speaking to Kivie): This is mother. You have been in Europe recently. Emily, you have a daughter.

Emily Kaplan: I have two daughters.

Fletcher: Tell your daughters that they are going to be all right. [Both daughters were expecting babies within a few weeks.]

Fletcher: There is a young woman here who says she wants to talk with mother. Her name is Mary and she has been over here several years. [Mrs. Shapiro had had a daughter who passed over many years ago. Neither the Kaplans nor I knew about this.] Mary says, "I came over here when I was very young but I have grown up and am very happy in my work here. Mother, I love you dearly and am so happy to have this first chance to tell you so and give you a short message. Also tell my father that I am proud of his work as a doctor and that he is doing much good."

Fletcher: There is an ancestor here named Macoski.

Mrs. Shapiro: I had ancestors with that name.

Fletcher: Mrs. Kaplan says, "I want very much to build up knowledge of how to communicate with you now that we have begun this contact. Give my love to Marion."

Kivie: Is my father there?

Fletcher: Yes, your father is here. There is a man here who has the same name as you. [This delighted Kivie, for he had been named after his grandfather, a famous European rabbi.]

Kivie: But my grandfather knew no English, so how can he communicate with us?

Harlow: Do you use languages over there?

Fletcher: No. We use thought transference, but it is too difficult to explain to you in the earth plane. When we communicate with you we have to use the language we know. Rabbi Kaplan transmits his thoughts and I pass them on to you in English.

The remainder of that sitting was concerned with intimate messages that would serve no purpose to be reported here.

As remarkable as that sitting was to the Kaplans and to the unannounced Mrs. Shapiro, my first meeting with Ford five years earlier was even stranger, because I came in on him as a complete stranger only five minutes after telephoning him for an appointment, and Fletcher brought me myriad messages from persons who were complete unknowns to Ford.

Marion and I were in New York, and when we had finished our business we both agreed that we should meet this famous medium. On the chance that we might find him in, we impulsively went to his hotel and called him from the lobby. I told him of my interest in the paranormal and that my wife and a friend, Anne Wiggin, were with me. Could we see him? He said that he had a cold and was not feeling well but because we had come down from Northampton he would see us. In a minute we stepped out of the elevator and he greeted us—three complete strangers whose names he had never heard until a few minutes before.

In that hour's meeting on December 5, 1952, Fletcher brought us messages from seven personalities, six of whom we had known well. It was the first that we were unable to identify. He said he was a former relative named John Stafford, but we know of no person in the family by that name, although my wife's maiden name is Stafford and our son is named John Stafford Harlow.

Then in quick succession came several persons who had been close to me during their earthly lives. They identified themselves so accurately by name, occupation, and personal connection with us that it would be difficult to disbelieve them. They included:

Cass Reed, a classmate of mine at Union Seminary whose marriage service I had performed.

Shepherd Knapp, a Congregational minister in Worcester, Massachusetts, for whom I had preached many times. He said, "You have a great help in your wife, a help that was lacking in my life." And I remembered that he had led a lonely bachelor's life.

My mother, who said, "You are going to have a wonderful Christmas with your three Carols. As you know, I too, was a Carol. Make the most of this Christmas, for next year you will be far over the ocean." Her message was astounding with accuracies that were known only in close family circles. Her reference to the "three Carols" was especially significant, because Mother's name was Caroline and the Carols who did join us at Christmas that year were our daughter, Ruth Carol, and our two grandchildren, Linda Carol and Jean Carol. And her year-ahead prophecy about our being "far over the ocean" the following Christmas was also accurate: we were in Athens.

The most convincing message came from Mary Hussey, a member of the department of religion at Mount Holyoke College whom we had known slightly and who had died suddenly the previous summer. She said, "I want you to tell Paul something for me. Tell him that I regretted leaving so suddenly with my work unfinished. It was in the classics. Tell him I am proud of him and his work and will try to help him find someone to finish my work."

It was perfectly clear to me who Paul was. He was Paul Williams, a very close friend of mine who was chairman of Mount Holyoke's department of religion. When we returned to Northampton I went over to see Paul and asked him what Mary Hussey had been doing at the time of her death. He said, "She was translating some cuneiform tablets and had not finished her work. We are trying to get someone to complete it, as the publishers want it as soon as possible."

I suppose it is possible that some of Arthur Ford's, or Fletcher's, messages could be explained on the basis of telepathy, but if so the telepathic ability involved seems as remarkable as Fletcher himself. But even granting telepathy we must exclude the Mary Hussey message: Arthur Ford did not know Paul Williams or Mary Hussey; and none of us in that room knew of her work in the classics.

Perhaps the greatest feat of Arthur Ford—although it required no more effort on his part than did bringing me messages from my mother—was his instrumentality in bringing an other-world message from the most skeptical of them all, Harry Houdini.

When he died in 1926 at the age of fifty-two, Harry Houdini was probably the world's greatest magician, an escape artist beyond parallel. He had demonstrated his skill by escaping from almost all of the escapeproof prisons of the world, and once he allowed experts to bind him securely with rope, nail him in a packing case which was then bound with steel bands, and then drop him into the Hudson River. In less than a minute he popped to the surface.

For years before his death he devoted much time to psychic phenomena, almost all of it exposing the frauds that are almost certain to be found in any subject so emotional. But he came to feel that all psychic experiences were frauds without exception. He was certainly a hostile witness. As a member of a committee investigating the Margery-Walter phenomena he alienated other members because it soon became apparent that he had made up his mind that Margery was a fraud even before the investigation began.

But his mind was not completely closed. He had asked his mother to send him a secret code word after her death. If he received this, he said, he would be convinced of the survival of personality. It never came in his lifetime. And before his death he and his wife, Beatrice, evolved an intricate coding system that only they knew. Whoever died first would use that code to send evidence of survival. The magician was the first to go.

Arthur Ford came into the picture suddenly and without warning. In the sixteen months following the death of Houdini countless messages were reported as coming from the magician. None of them was correct, and Beatrice Houdini denounced them all.

But one evening in February 1928 when Arthur Ford was giving a sitting to a group of friends, Fletcher reported that he had a message from "the mother of Harry Weiss, known as Houdini."

Houdini's mother reported that she had been attempting for years to transmit their secret code word to her son but had been unable to do so. Beatrice Houdini, she said, would verify the word and once the verification was completed Houdini himself would send his coded message to his wife. Fletcher then transmitted the word "Forgive" and Mrs. Houdini was notified. Publicly she said the message was "the sole communication received among thousands up to this time that contained the one secret key word known only to Houdini, his mother, and myself." And to Ford she wrote, "...had this been given him [Houdini] while he was still alive it would have changed the entire course of his life."

It was nine months later that Fletcher brought the first of a series of eight other Houdini messages. When he finished ten weeks later, Ford had a jumbled series of words that now needed decoding. The ten-word message, "Rosabelle answer tell pray answer look tell answer answer tell," was sent to Mrs. Houdini, who immediately recognized the significance of the first word, "Rosabelle." Following the instructions forwarded to her by Fletcher through Arthur Ford, Mrs. Houdini attended a sitting with Arthur Ford, and in the presence of a United Press reporter, a close personal friend, and an associate editor of *Scientific American*, Houdini and his wife, with Fletcher as the intermediary, decoded the message. It read: "Rosabelle, believe."

That day Mrs. Houdini signed a statement for the world to read: "Regardless of any statements made to the contrary, I wish to declare that the message, in its entirety, and in the agreed sequence, given to me by Arthur Ford, is the correct message prearranged between Mr. Houdini and myself."

Even today there are those who say, "Well, if there's anything to this psychic business, what about Houdini? He never got through to his wife as he promised, and if he can't get through, no one can." But Houdini *did* get through if we can believe his wife, and what possible basis is there for accusing her of deliberate fraud? And to turn the phrase—if Houdini can get through, then others can.

My friendship and experiences with Arthur Ford, including his telling me of the Houdini messages, have left me greatly indebted to him. His calm autobiography, *Nothing So Strange*, reveals his character and his careful approach to the mysterious results of his great gift. And I can never forget what he once told a group of us: "God and immortality are bound up together. No God; no immortality. The two words belong to a family of ideas, the noblest group of conceptions ever conceived in the mind of man."

And these words in turn remind me of those of Joseph Addison: "If there's a power above us, (And that there is all nature cries aloud through all her works), he must delight in virtue."

16

Researcher in Absentia

Like so many doctoral dissertations, the one written by Dr. John F. Thomas will never compete with *Peyton Place* on the best-seller lists. Even its title is somewhat discouraging: *An Evaluative and Methodological Study of the Mental Content of Certain Trance Phenomena*.

But to the scholar interested in the paranormal, it contains some of the most fascinating tables, charts, footnotes, and graphs ever bound between hard covers.

I was introduced to this 319-page scholarly work by its author when I met him during a summer of teaching in North Carolina. Like his dissertation, which was published under the title *Beyond Normal Cognition*, Dr. Thomas is mild, cautious, and scholarly. He does not easily leap to conclusions, but his findings easily make their own.

This careful researcher was led to psychic investigation in middle life, after a long career as a chief administrator of the Detroit, Michigan, school system. Until the death of his wife, Ethel, in April 1926, he had little interest in the paranormal. But three months later he had embarked on a series of experiments that were to last for nine years, send him to Duke University for a doctor of philosophy degree in psychology, and result in some of the most remarkable psychic evidence yet gathered.

He started rather casually with what he called "Two experiments... with no attempt to conceal my name." They were séances, or sittings, with mediums who fell into a trance-like sleep in a normally lighted room, without the darkened room or red-light requirements of some psychics. The result was the reception of sixty-two correct pieces of information, many of them concerning his dead wife and some concerning his parents, who had been dead for several years. His analytical mind recognized that the record far exceeded what could be expected by chance, and he went forward with further research.

He approached William McDougall, professor of psychology at Duke University for guidance in his work, and soon had the help not only of McDougall but of J. B. and Louisa Rhine. He became a candidate for a doctor's degree and returned to lecture rooms and laboratories in order to prepare for the task he had set for himself. He had decided to answer the question: Are there instances of supernormal information?

As a beginning he had 149 personal sittings with the famous Boston sensitive Mrs. Minnie M. Soule, and in addition he sent his secretary to her for 217 other sessions when he was unable to attend. Then, in co-operation with the British college of Psychic Science and the English Society for Psychical Research, he arranged for 134 sittings in England with some of Britain's most respected psychics. He attended only nineteen of these; the others were recorded for him by hired stenographers, some of whom knew nothing about Thomas or his affairs. In other words, out of 500 sittings he attended only 168 himself; the others, 332 of them, were proxy sittings.

In his dissertation he reports on 1720 verifiable statements of fact that were received over the years from twenty-two different mediums. Many of these statements concerned his married life, his activities after his wife's death, and the life of his wife before she had married Thomas—a period about which Thomas was frequently uninformed. Of the 1720 different statements of fact, 92 per cent proved to be correct, and some of them were statements about which Dr. Thomas had no knowledge at the time he received them, but was later able to verify.

The cold statistical analysis of the dissertation conceals the exciting drama of the communications, but as I talked with Dr. Thomas about some of the incidents the mediums had reported I could not help becoming excited. For example, at one sitting his dead wife identified herself by giving remarkably precise details of her funeral. She was buried wearing an Italian necklace of polished cream-colored stone that had been given her by a son. A description of the necklace as transmitted by an English medium included ten specific points—such as the color, the shape of the stones, the length—and nine of these points were correct.

During another proxy session in Kent, England, a communication was received concerning the Thomases' summer home on Lake Huron at

Lexington, Michigan. The description included the boat landing, the two seats near it, and a rocky path. Of the twenty-one points of actual description twenty-one were correct—a 100-percent score.

Often Mrs. Thomas gave messages concerning her husband's recent day-to-day life. When a research observer, present at one of the proxy sessions, asked of the spirit control, "Has she [Mrs. Thomas] been watching her gentleman lately?" the answer was, "Such a joke. Has he been thinking of fishes quite lately—a lot of fishes?" Dr. Thomas records that at the time of this sitting he was making preparations for the opening of the fishing season.

Further remarks recorded at this session, with Dr. Thomas' later remarks, follow:

> *Mrs. Thomas:* Quite lately I have been concerned with some alterations and additions to a building.
> *Dr. Thomas' remarks:* At the time this record was taken we were talking of building a garage.
> *Mrs. Thomas:* He hasn't been doing it so much as planning it.
> *Dr. Thomas' remarks;* We had planned it, but never built it.

At one London session Mrs. Thomas sent a message to her husband: "Thank him very much for what he did with regard to some movement of a picture which I didn't like. . . . Don't forget to tell him that I like the house, the change in the picture, and the way he has been conducting things in the last five months." Dr. Thomas noted: "A striking point here is the statement that the movement is of 'a picture that I didn't like.' She decidedly did not like this picture."

Other messages also concerned the homey things of family life—the millstone they bought and placed in the front yard as a door step, and the difference of opinion about what color to paint the shutters—tiny, almost insignificant happenings in a normal, this-world life, but startling, almost irrefutable evidence of survival when delivered as Dr. Thomas received them.

We must remember that Dr. Thomas' work was accepted as an original research project in partial fulfillment for a doctor of philosophy degree from a university of high standing. Of the man, Professor McDougall writes: "Dr. Thomas has shown himself so conscientious, so self-critical, so well able and so well disposed to discount the effect upon his work of any desire to prove his wife's survival, that the possiblity of its being a distorting influence, being well recognized by him, must have served, I think, to make him the more careful and impartial in his procedures."

Shortly after the Thomas report was made public, the New York *Times* science editor reported, "If we assume fraud we must also assume a gigantic conspiracy which was carried on for seven years on both sides of the Atlantic at an appalling expense and which involved twenty-two sensitives and scores of acquaintances, friends and close relatives."

Writing cautiously and conservatively, Dr. Thomas himself says, "...the results of psychical research favor an interpretation of the universe that views it as something other than 'aimless cosmic weather,' and that affords all those who think that there are ultimate nonmaterial values at the heart of things an increasingly broadening base of evidence."

But he told me that as a result of his experiences he had become certain of the survival of his wife, and that her memory and personality continued.

I agreed with him. Only a supernormal explanation is adequate to explain such communications; no other intelligence except that of Mrs. Thomas could have been the source of those messages.

Dr. Thomas' experiences and his patient and thorough study of this one question—had his wife survived?—should open a great door of hope to many unbelieving minds. The work of Dr. Thomas should bring much comfort to those who cry, as did the father of the epileptic child (Mark 9:24), "Lord, I believe; help thou mine unbelief."

17

"Nothing Shall Be Impossible unto You"

During the past decade there has been a strong revival of interest in spiritual healing. In fact the movement has attracted so much interest that the Protestant Episcopal Church, which has given much time and thought to this phase of psychical experience, calls it a renaissance.

There is a strong Biblical background for this healing power, especially in St. Luke. It is quite obvious that to the Beloved Physician the act of healing was of paramount importance in the life of the early church. It was always present in the ministry of Jesus, the greatest spiritual healer in history, and it continued in the apostolic era. But faith was one condition stressed by Jesus; even he could not heal where faith was lacking.

We read in Matthew 13:58: "And he did not mighty works there because of their unbelief." Later in Matthew, when the disciples asked Jesus why they had been powerless to cure a stricken child, Jesus replied: "...because of your unbelief; for verily I say unto you, If ye have faith as a grain of mustard seed, ye shall say unto this mountain, Remove hence to yonder place; and it shall remove, and nothing shall be impossible unto you."

Where there was faith there was healing. St. Luke tells us how Jesus cured leprosy, palsy, dropsy, and a multitude of diseases. In Acts 14:8 we read that "there sat a certain man at Lystra, impotent in his feet, being a cripple from his mother's womb, who never had walked. The same heard

Paul speak; who steadfastly beholding him, and perceiving that he had faith to be healed, said with a loud voice, Stand upright on thy feet. And he leaped and walked."

Actually, so far as healing is concerned, the Christian Church has changed little in the two thousand years since these cures were effected. In almost every church we find the congregation offering prayers for the sick and disabled. The Roman Catholic Church has established shrines at sites where divine healings have taken place; and at such shrines as Lourdes, Protestant physicians have investigated and testified to numerous healings which could not be explained other than by supernormal intervention. Such healings have not been limited to cases of psychosomatic illness, sickness caused by the mind, but have included cures of cancer, broken bones, and destroyed tissues.

Only recently my good friend Alson J. Smith, a Congregational minister, summed up the revived interest in this basic Christian concept: "Doctors of all faiths bring their 'incurable' patients to Lourdes in increasing numbers. Seminars on spiritual healing are held under the auspices of the Laymen's Movement at Wainwright House, Rye, N.Y., at Dr. John Sutherland Bonnell's Fifth Avenue Presbyterian church, and at many other churches.... The National Council of Churches has conducted a survey among the clergy which shows that 43 per cent of America's Protestant ministers claim to have had some experience with spiritual healing. The Protestant Episcopal diocese of Pittsburgh has established a Healing Commission. In Great Britain, more than fourteen hundred clergymen study healing methods through the Churches' Fellowship for Psychical Studies. In hundreds of churches throughout the United States, Canada and Great Britain, 'prayer groups' pray at the same time for the healing of selected lists of sick people."

Now this is not Christian Science. The spiritual healing I am talking about does not ignore the help which comes from hospitals, physicians, and medicine. These things are the instruments that God uses to bring us health, and we cannot ignore them. In the succinct words of the phrase carved into the walls of one medical school, "We dress the wound; God heals it."

Let me cite an example told me by a friend who was involved. Not long ago a young widow fell from a fourth-story window and impaled herself on a picket fence. Photographers snapped pictures of what they thought was a dead woman. An ambulance doctor administered a blood transfusion, but at the hospital the staff gave her little hope for recovery. Then a nurse, a Roman Catholic assigned to the case, began to pray, and she was urged to continue her prayers.

Some slight hope began to emerge, but when a bone specialist was called in he said surgery would be futile. "She might live, but she will never walk again," he said. But the prayers continued, and the patient began to gain a new spiritual insight. Two years later the bone specialist announced to the woman, "My child, you have a perfect body. This is miraculous."

It is possible of course to fill thousands of pages with documented accounts of healing that took place beyond the scope of medical knowledge. But none of the accounts is more remarkable than the record of Edgar Cayce (pronounced "Casey"), an uneducated Virginia photographer who for forty-four years diagnosed and prescribed treatment for more than ten thousand persons, many of them given up as incurable by medical specialists.

I never met Edgar Cayce, but I feel I know him through two close friends who investigated him shortly before his death in 1945 and wrote about him. Thomas Sugrue's biography of Cayce, *There Is a River*, tells in great detail the amazing work of one of the greatest healers in modern history, and Sherwood Eddy included Cayce in his book *You Will Survive After Death*.

Cayce's first indication that he had any psychic inclination came when he was a schoolboy, studying his spelling, on a small Kentucky farm. He was an intolerably poor speller, a generally poor student, and simply could not remember what he had read despite conscientious effort. One night he asked his father, by then impatient with his son's progress, if he could "sleep on" his speller for a few minutes. His father agreed, and young Edgar closed the book and napped for a few minutes. When he woke he not only knew his spelling lesson but could spell any word in the book.

This was his first experience. When he grew older he was hired by a wholesaler when he demonstrated that he knew every item, page by page, in the firm's catalogue. He had memorized the volume as he had his speller, by "sleeping on it." When he was twenty-one he became mute, unable to speak for some unknown reason. A New York City specialist treated him through hypnosis—certainly a daring treatment in those days—and, learning of his patient's psychic abilities, suggested he might cure himself.

Young Cayce tried, and succeeded. Having learned from his physician the method of self-hypnosis, he placed himself in light trance, diagnosed his trouble, and cured himself by autosuggestion. From that point on he began to apply his gifts to helping others. Word of his ability spread, and soon doctors, baffled by patients who did not respond to treatment, began to call on him for help. Cayce discovered that he need not see the patient to diagnose the trouble and prescribe treatment. It made no difference if he had never heard of the patient, and many of his readings were made from letters sent to him by persons hundreds of miles away. Before each reading he would bow his head for a few moments of silent prayer, place himself in mild trance, and dictate his findings.

Often his diagnoses were phrased in technical medical terms understandable only to men trained in the medical profession, terms which he did not know or understand when out of his trance.

Sherwood Eddy recounts the results of a questionnaire he sent to a dozen physicians who had worked with Cayce over the years. The doctors reported that out of 150 cases brought to their attention Cayce's diagnoses had been 80 per cent correct. Some of their comments included: "He is highly accurate in diagnosis and beneficial in treatments, not quite understandable in a layman." "His readings are wonderful. I presume you would call it supernormal. I think he has the power to contact a higher vibration, or that which is eternal." "This man certainly has something. Yes, I would call it supernormal."

At the risk of stretching credulity to its breaking point I now move on to the strange case of Dr. Benjamin Rush, who treated and cured three friends of mine more than 125 years after his death.

I do not know what to think of Dr. Rush and the psychic group he once visited. I cannot explain and I do not understand. But I can report what I have been told, and I can vouch for the honesty, intelligence, and integrity of my sources; it is unthinkable that these friends of mine would be involved in a hoax, a fraud, or a lie.

To receive more meaning from the Rush cures it is necessary to review the background of this native Philadelphian who was both patriot and physician. Benjamin Rush was born in 1745, graduated from Princeton College, and studied medicine in Philadelphia, London, Edinburgh, and Paris. In 1769 he was appointed professor of chemistry at the College of Philadelphia, and he was the author of many articles for medical journals. An ardent Whig, he was elected a member of the Continental Congress and signed the Declaration of Independence. In 1785 he established the Philadelphia Dispensary, the first in the nation; and in 1787 he was a member of the Pennsylvania convention which ratified the federal constitution.

After he retired from political life he became professor of the theory and practice of medicine at the Philadelphia Medical College. In 1793, when an epidemic of yellow fever swept his city, he was believed to have saved the lives of six thousand persons. His practice became so large that he treated as many as one hundred patients a day, even talking with them while he ate his meals. He died on April 19, 1813. Today his name is kept alive by the University of Chicago in its Rush Graduate School of Medicine.

And for most purposes this is the end of Benjamin Rush, patriot, politician, and devoted physician.

But a few years ago a group of psychic investigators meeting regularly in New York City were visited by a spirit purporting to be Dr. Benjamin Rush. He told this group that he now was much more skilled than when he practiced his profession in Philadelphia, and that he was willing to treat some patients. However, speaking almost as if he had consulted the American Medical Association before appearing, he said that he must insist on either of two conditions: 1) the patient must already be beyond help by competent physicians, or 2) the patient must be too poor to pay for medical attention.

A short time later a woman friend of mine, afflicted with incurable cancer and considered a terminal case by five cancer specialists, heard of Dr. Rush's offer. Obviously she qualified, and because she certainly had nothing to lose, she went to New York and attended a sitting with the medium who had previously brought the message from the early American doctor.

At this sitting Rush listened to what she had to say, and like any modern specialist he said he wanted to consider the case after making an examination. He instructed his patient to go to bed early the following night, to place herself in a state of complete repose and confidence, and to pray. He said that he would then make an exploratory examination of her and that she was to return the following night to the séance group for his report.

She told me, "That night I followed his directions explicitly. I prayed fervently and felt great peace; it was as if some supernormal power enveloped me."

At the séance the following night Dr. Rush announced brusquely that he would take the case. He instructed her to repeat his orders of the preceding night. He emphasized calm repose and prayer. While she was asleep, he said, he would remove the cancer; for the next week she was to remain quietly in bed, taking nourishment to keep up her strength and using prayer to comfort her.

That night she passed into a coma. "When I woke in the morning I knew I had been healed," she told me. "The only sign of an operation was a small spot of blood on the bed sheet."

Within a week she was able to dress herself, and a few days later she went to her doctor for an examination. He checked her thoroughly and pronounced her entirely free of cancer. "It's almost miraculous," he said. The cancer has never returned and she is now in better health than she has known in years.

Some years later I was preaching at an Eastern women's college, and one night during a lively blizzard I sat before a roaring fire with the college chaplain. He mentioned that he was writing his master's thesis on the topic of psychical research. This of course led us into a long and most interesting exchange of experiences. As we talked I mentioned Dr. Rush and the incurable cancer that he had healed in my friend.

I rather expected him to scoff, but to my utter amazement the chaplain said, "Yes, I know. I know about him and the work he is doing. In fact he cured my wife of very serious stomach ulcers. She was suffering great pain, and several doctors were completely unable to do anything. Then when we were in deep despair of ever getting any help we heard of the New York group which was in contact with Dr. Rush. We went there; Dr. Rush gave my wife several treatments; and she is completely cured. No, I don't need to be convinced; I know. We have evidence of a spirit with supernormal power who is interested in helping people who are sick."

Later I received another Dr. Rush testimonial—this one from a most unlikely source, a college psychology professor. Often, perhaps as a result of their training and occupation, psychologists are stubborn and biased when it comes to paranormal occurrences. They go far past the healthy skepticism of the scientist and seem to close their minds to things that cannot be explained in their own terms. But there are exceptions, and this one was a magnificent exception. Here was a psychologist who admitted that Dr. Benjamin Rush, dead for more than a century, had cured his wife of gallstones after a competent physician had given up the case.

There seems to be no doubt that prayer—and remember that in the fantastic Dr. Rush cases he asked his patients to pray—often has extraordinary therapeutic power. Edgar Cayce always prayed before each reading; the Episcopal Church is encouraging its clergy to hold regular services at which prayers for healing are offered.

If we believe that God's healing grace is an active presence available to all who turn to Him in faith, if we make prayer a constant habit, and silent meditation a daily practice, then we can make these words of Whittier's no longer merely a beautiful poem but a reality to be accepted:

> The healing of his seamless dress is by our beds of pain;
> We touch him in life's throng and press, and we are whole again.

18

Psychic Experiences in the New Testament

Whenever we turn to the great writings of the past, whether to the Egyptian *Book of the Dead*, to the Greek tragedies of the Golden Age of Athens, or to the Latin writers of ancient Rome, we find constant references to psychic experiences.

There is, however, no book which has borne witness to survival so much as has the Bible; in the Old Testament we find many psychic experiences, and in the New Testament even more. Both volumes constantly assert that above us, about us, and within us is a vast spiritual universe and that we are in close, vital, and wondrous relationship with it.

At the very center of Christianity we come face to face not with an ancient tale about a crucified prophet but with the dynamic influence of a living personality. Jesus has not been merely a memory.

As a child I was taught to accept the Bible as the inspired word of God, never to be questioned whether it dealt with physical laws, historical events, or social and spiritual matters. The resurrection stories, I was told, must be accepted exactly as they were written in the Gospels.

Later, in my college years, I went through a period of great confusion and doubt. It was not the scientific errors in the Scripture that bothered me so much as it was the ethical and spiritual attitude I found in the Old Testament. Massacre, polygamy, murder, war, slavery, and countless other evils were pictured as approved by God—often ordered by Him.

The utterly primitive interpretation of creation undermined my childhood faith, but this defection was mild compared with my shock at discovering so many un-Christlike concepts in the Old Testament.

Then I was fortunate enough to take a course with Harry Emerson Fosdick at Union Theological Seminary, a course called "The Modern Approach to the Bible." It was as if a veil had been torn from my mind and the Bible restored to me as a living book to be interpreted in the light of the age in which each book was written.

But even then I considered many of the New Testament stories as tales based on wishful thinking, enlarged over the centuries, and not to be taken as based on actual experiences. The parables—the message of Jesus—shone with splendor and held me with unlimited devotion, but I could not accept many of the historic events in the Gospels.

And then came a great revelation to my mind: I began to interpret these events in terms of psychic experiences and they came to have significance and meaning.

Surely no one can read the Epistles of St. Paul or the Book of Acts, which tells of St. Paul's conversion, without admitting that here we have reports of psychic experiences.

No other man had such influence on the spread of Christianity as did St. Paul. A trained religious leader among the Jews, a fanatical persecutor of the early Christians, he became the first great missionary of this faith he had persecuted, and a martyr for the Christ he had once hated.

In Paul's own story, as told in his great defense before King Agrippa, in Acts 26 we read: "At midday, O king, I saw in the way a light from heaven, above the brightness of the sun, shining round about me, and them which journeyed with me. And when we were all fallen to the earth, I heard a voice speaking to me in the Hebrew tongue, Saul, Saul, why persecutist thou me? It is hard for thee to kick against the pricks. And I said, Who art thou, Lord? And he said, I am Jesus whom thou persecutist. But rise, and stand upon thy feet: for I have appeared unto thee for this purpose, to make thee a minister and a witness both of these things which thou hast seen, and of those things in which I will appear unto thee....Whereupon, O king Agrippa, I was not disobedient unto the heavenly vision."

Here is a psychic experience which was to shape all history, the importance of which cannot be overestimated. It transformed Saul of Tarsus, educated as a rabbi, into Paul the missionary—a witness to the truth and universal nature of the Christian gospel.

For this cause Paul, in his own words, suffered much. "Of the Jews five times received I forty stripes save one," says Paul. "Thrice I was beaten with rods, once was I stoned, thrice I suffered shipwreck, a night and a day I have been in the deep; In journeyings often, in perils of waters, in perils of robbers, in perils of my own countrymen, in perils by the heathen, in perils in the city, in perils in the wilderness, in perils in the sea, in perils among false brethren; in weariness and painfulness, in watchings often, in hunger and thirst, in fastings often, in cold and nakedness. Beside those things that are without, that which cometh unto me daily, the care of all the churches." (II Corinthians 11:24-28)

Now a man does not endure such things without cause. He does not face the scorn and attacks of his own people, whom he loves, or of the Gentiles, for whom he felt such great concern, without an experience so transforming, so real, so convincing that his entire mind and heart and soul become convinced of the reality and truth of that experience. It was Paul who first carried the gospel over into Greece and later to Rome.

Let us then raise the question as to just what did happen on that road to Damascus back in A.D. 31 that changed Saul, a dedicated rabbi and enemy of all Christians, into St. Paul the apostle and missionary to the Gentile world on behalf of Christ.

Now the Book of Acts was written about forty years after the events described; that is the same length of time that has elapsed since I went to France with the American Expeditionary Force in World War I. How very clear and vivid those months and experiences in France are to my mind today. Sights and sounds, faces and voices come back to me across the years in distinct and accurate memories.

There is some difference to be found in the three separate accounts of St. Paul's experience. In Acts 9, as told by Luke, we read that the men with Paul "stood speechless, hearing the voice, but beholding no man." In this version only Paul saw the great light and beheld the vision. The others heard only the voice. This could be interpreted as a subjective experience in so far as the vision is concerned, but the voice was a more objective experience, being shared with his companions.

In Paul's address to the crowd in Jerusalem he says that "they that were with me beheld indeed the light, but they heard not the voice of him that spake to me." (Acts 22:9)

It is difficult to explain this experience as merely subjective, an hallucination unshared by others in the company. Luke seems to be aware that such an explanation would occur to those who heard the story, and as a physician he was fully cognizant that such an explanation would be acceptable to many minds, especially since the vision came at midday in the heat of the sun. But both Luke and Paul were sure that this was no hallucination. Paul staked his very life on this vision. Luke, a Christian physician, devoted to the truth, and a companion of Paul, was as convinced as Paul that this was a supernatural visitation.

Another reference to Paul's vision may be found in his letter to the Corinthians (I Corinthians 15:3-8): "For I delivered unto you first of all that which I also received, how that Christ died for our sins according to the scriptures: and that he was buried, and that he rose again the third day according to the scriptures: and that he was seen of Peter, then of the twelve; after that he was seen of about five hundred brethren at once; of whom the greater part remain unto this present but some are fallen asleep. And that, he was seen of James; then of all the apostles. *And last of all he was seen of me*, that am not meet to be called an apostle, because I persecuted the church of God." (Italics mine.)

Now Paul never met Jesus in the flesh so far as we know. Did he, then, stake his life, his reputation, his honor, on something which he himself doubted to be a true revelation?

It is evident from the account that follows the vision that it had a strong psychological effect on Paul, for there is no indication that the light blinded his companions as it did him. In Damascus a devout Christian named Ananias put his hands on Paul's eyes and, we read, "immediately there fell from his eyes as it had been scales; and he received sight forthwith, and arose, and was baptized." (Acts 9:18)

For three days he had been blind. Now he saw. It is an interesting fact that it was then a common belief that it took three days for the soul to separate itself from the physical body at death. And in this experience the enemy of Christ died and the missionary of the cross was born.

I do not say that on that road to Damascus Paul actually saw Christ and heard him speak. What is important is that as a result of that experience Paul's whole life was transformed. I myself do believe that it was a psychic experience and that Christ was the *source* and *cause* of the vision; that it was an actual and vivid vision in which Christ was able to manifest himself to Paul and make known his mission to him.

In the record we come on other psychic experiences in Paul's life. Outstanding is the vision as told in Acts 16:9: "And a vision appeared to Paul at night; There stood a man of Macedonia, and prayed him, saying, Come over into Macedonia, and help us. And after he had seen the vision, immediately we endeavored to go into Macedonia, assuredly gathering that the Lord had called us to preach the gospel unto them." It was thus that the gospel was carried for the first time into Europe.

It is of no great significance to others that I have had a few very vivid psychic dreams in which my sister appeared to me and talked with me about very intimate matters concerning her family and children in the year following her death; it has significance only for me. But this dream of Paul's had significance for the whole of Europe and later for America. No one can study dreams, as Professor Hornell Hart and his wife have done, and about which they have written a book, and not arrive at the conclusion that there are dreams that seem to have a supernormal source and do convey a message.

In St. Paul's letter to the Corinthians we come on another statement that would indicate his sensitivity to psychic experiences. In II Corinthians 12:1-4 we read Paul's story. It is worth reading in full: "It is not expedient for me doubtless to glory. I will come to visions and revelations of the Lord. I knew a man in Christ above fourteen years ago, (whether in the body, I cannot tell; or whether out of the body, I cannot tell: God knoweth;) such an one caught up to the third heaven. And I knew such a man, (whether in the body, or out of the body, I cannot tell: God knoweth;) how he was caught up into paradise, and heard unspeakable words, which it is not lawful for a man to utter. Of such a one will I glory."

I know full well with what skepticism and even ridicule such an illustration will be met by those who claim that *all* such phenomena can be explained by psychological research and that such an experience is not a revelation from spiritual sources. But I believe that we are challenged "to love the Lord thy God with all thy *mind*" (Luke 10:27; italics mine). Blind faith was an expression of religion which Jesus attacked.

I hold that *thinking* is as much a religious duty as worship and praying. But I am also aware that reason has its limits and that as Dr. J. Arthur Hill points out, "If I ask a rationalist to prove to me his own existence, he will be unable to do so."

The warfare between science and religion has come to an end for most intelligent scholars, both scientists and religious leaders. In 1633 the congregation of prelates and cardinals passed a decree saying that "the doctrine that the earth is neither the center of the universe nor immovable, but moves with a daily rotation, is absurd, and both philosophically and theologically false." But truth has prevailed against even these hosts of ecclesiasticism.

I believe that in the experiences of Paul we have evidence of *direct spiritual revelation*. The means by which that vision comes—the psychological basis for the revelations—is not the important factor; what is important is that a transforming and inspiring *direction* is given to life. That God should be unable to touch our lives, as he did Jeremiah and Isaiah and Jesus, would make Him indeed a limited being. He has touched the lives of countless others—Thoreau, Emerson, Henry Ward Beecher, Schweitzer—and the lives of millions of unknown, through whom, like the clear panes of polished window, this goodness shines.

Leaving the letters of Paul and the records in the Book of Acts, let us turn to the Gospel narratives with their many psychic experiences.

Take, for example, the beautiful story in St. Luke of the angel chorus greeting the shepherds at the time of Jesus' birth. Is this merely an allegory? Or is it based on an actual experience? For nearly two thousand years Christians have acclaimed "the holy birth" in triumphant carols with such lines as:

> "Hark! the herald angels sing,"
> "While shepherds watched their flocks by night."
> "Angels from the realms of glory."
> "It came upon the midnight clear."
> "We hear the Christmas angels, the great glad tidings tell."

These carols lift our hearts nearer to heaven at Christmastime, but are we hypocrites as we sing them? Many of us are, but we need not be. Is it so difficult to believe that angels actually sang at Jesus' birth? For surely of all births none has meant so much to mankind as the birth of Jesus. Nor does it seem strange that His birth should have been accompanied by angelic hosts singing, "Peace on earth, good will to men."

Preceeding the birth of Jesus we have other stories of a psychic nature, such as the angel Gabriel first appearing to Zacharias to tell him about the birth of John the Baptist, and then going to Mary to tell her of Jesus' forthcoming birth (Luke 1:5-25).

At the time of Jesus' baptism we come again on psychic phenomena. In Matthew 3:13-17 we have both a clairvoyant and clairaudient experience: "Then cometh Jesus from Galilee to Jordan, unto John, to be baptized of him. But John forbade him, saying, I have need to be baptized of thee, and camest thou to me? And Jesus answering said unto him, Suffer it to be so now: for thus it becometh us to fulfill all righteousness. Then he suffered him. And Jesus, when he was baptized, went up straightway out of the water: and lo, the heavens were opened unto him, and he saw the Spirit of God descending like a dove, and lighting upon him: And lo, a voice from heaven saying, This is my beloved son, in whom I am well pleased."

And in Matthew 14:25 we have a levitation phenomenon: "And in the fourth watch of the night Jesus went unto them, walking on the sea."

Of the New Testament stories in which psychic phenomena appear none is more dramatic than the story of the Transfiguration. This experience is told in all three of the Synoptic Gospels—Matthew, Mark, and Luke—but it appears first in Mark 9:2-8, where we read: "And after six days Jesus taketh with him Peter, and James, and John, and bringeth them up into a high mountain apart by themselves; and he was transfigured before them; and his garments became glistening, exceeding white, so as no fuller on earth can whiten them. And there appeared unto them Elijah and Moses: and they were talking with Jesus. And Peter answereth and saith to Jesus, Rabbi, it is good for us to be here; and let us make three tabernacles; one for thee, and one for Moses, and one for Elijah. For he knew not what to answer; for they became sore afraid. And there came a cloud overshadowing them; and there came a voice out of the cloud, This is my beloved Son; hear ye him. And suddenly looking around about, they saw no one any more, save Jesus only with themselves."

This is clearly both a clairvoyant and clairaudient experience. Unless we discredit Mark's account, we cannot say it is allegory. Something must have happened on that hilltop which left a profound and lasting impression on those three disciples who shared the wonder of that hour with Jesus. Mark certainly discussed this experience with the three witnesses—Peter, James, and John—and found that their description of what happened coincided in important details.

It is easy for the unbelieving skeptic to ascribe the entire phenomenon to hypnotic trance or to subjective causes. But for those of us who have made a thorough and scientific study of such phenomena, it is by no means a satisfactory or rational explanation of the experience. For some of us have also seen spirit forms in "glistening white," and we have heard voices when we were by no means in a trance or subject to hallucinations. This mountaintop experience as related to three of the Gospels bears all the marks of a true psychic experience.

When we come to the mystery of the Resurrection we are confronted with the most stupendous event in all of history.

Although St. Paul makes no reference to the birth of Jesus, and although the mother of Jesus isn't even mentioned in any letter of St. Paul's, when it comes to the Resurrection he knows no bounds for his conviction that here is the central event in history. Note his words: "And if Christ be not risen, then is our preaching vain, and your faith is also vain. Yea, and we are found false witnesses of God: because we have testified of God that he raised up Christ; whom he raised not up, if so be that the dead rise not. For if the dead rise not, then is not Christ raised: and if Christ be not raised, your faith is vain...if in this life only we have hope in Christ, we are of all men most miserable. But now is Christ risen from the dead" (I Corinthians 15:14-20).

A study of psychical phenomena throws much light upon the whole Resurrection story. One cannot be acquainted with this field without concluding that the dawn of Christianity is associated with psychic phenomena on an unprecedented scale. Not to understand this closes the door to insight into accounts of the Resurrection.

The main events as told by the writers are these: Jesus, after His crucifixion and death, was placed in a tomb. Early the following day three women came to the tomb with the intent of anointing the body of Jesus with spices, a custom universal in Palestine at that time. These women were Mary Magdalene, whom Jesus had befriended; Mary, the mother of James; and Salome. That these women had no expectation of a risen Jesus is quite evident in the story.

They found the stone of the sepulchre rolled away, and here we have different accounts as to what they saw. In Luke we are told that "two men stood by them in dazzling apparel; and as they were affrighted and bowed down their faces to the earth, they said unto them, Why seek ye the living among the dead? He is not here, but is risen." Mark, however, speaks of only one young man, "sitting on the right side, arrayed in a white robe; and they were amazed." And his account closes with, "And they fled from the tomb; for trembling and astonishment had come upon them." Matthew records that "they departed quickly from the tomb with fear and great joy, and ran to bring his disciples word."

We then read that Peter and John ran to the tomb and they saw the linen clothes used in wrapping a body for burial. Of John we read, "...he saw, and believed."

This account in John is followed by the experience of Mary: "But Mary stood without at the sepulchre weeping; and as she wept, she stooped down, and looked into the sepulchre, and seeth two angels in white sitting, the one at the head, the other at the feet, where the body of Jesus had lain. And they say unto her, Woman, why weepest thou? She saith unto them, Because they have taken away my Lord, and I know not where they have laid him. And when she had thus said, she turned herself back, and saw Jesus standing, and knew not that it was Jesus. Jesus saith unto her, Woman, why weepest thou? Whom seekest thou? She, supposing him to be the gardener, saith unto him, Sir, if thou have borne him hence, tell me where thou hast laid him, and I will take him away. Jesus saith unto her,

Mary. She turned herself, and saith unto him. Rabboni; which is Master. Jesus saith unto her, Touch me not; for I am not yet ascended to my Father: but go to my brethren, and say unto them, I ascend unto my Father: and to your Father; to my God and to your God. Mary Magdalene came and told the disciples that she had seen the Lord, and that he had spoken these things unto her." (John 20:11-18)

Although Mary Magdalene is included among the women at the tomb in the Synoptic Gospels this is the only record of a personal experience face to face with Jesus in the garden.

Numerous other psychic experiences took place following the Resurrection. Both Mark and Luke tell us of the appearance of Jesus to two of the disciples as they walked to the village of Emmaus. A stranger joined them while they were discussing the Crucifixion and the startling news of the Resurrection. They did not recognize Jesus until, when they had arrived at their destination, they invited Him into the house to break bread. Suddenly "their eyes were opened, and they knew him; and he vanished out of their sight." They reported the experience to the disciples gathered in Jerusalem. (Luke 24:13-35)

Perhaps no appearance of Jesus after the Resurrection has been given more thought than when He appeared to the disciples gathered in Jerusalem. This story is told by both the writers of St. Luke and St. John. (Luke 24:36-43. John 20:19-23)

In the version given by Luke we read, "And as they spake these things, he himself stood in the midst of them, and saith unto them, peace be unto you. But they were terrified and affrighted, and supposed they had seen a spirit. And he said unto them, Why are ye troubled? and wherefore do questionings arise in your heart? See my hands and my feet, that it is I myself; handle me, and see; for a spirit hath not flesh and bones, as ye behold me having. And when he had said this, he showed them his hands and his feet. And while they still disbelieved for joy, and wondered, he said unto them, Have ye here anything to eat? And they gave him a piece of broiled fish. And he took it, and ate before them."

In the account given in St. John we have an interesting sequel to this event. According to the writer of the Fourth Gospel, "Thomas, one of the twelve, called the Twin, was not with them when Jesus came. So the other disciples told him, 'We have seen the Lord.' But he said unto them, 'Unless I see in his hands the print of the nails, and place my finger in the print of the nails, and place my hand on his side, I will not believe.' " And so through all future history he became known as "Doubting Thomas." What a host of others have joined company with him in this!

John continues: "Eight days later, his disciples were again in the house, and Thomas was with them. The doors were shut, and Jesus came and stood among them, and said, 'Peace be unto you.' Then he said to Thomas, 'Put your finger here, and see my hands: and put your hand, and place it in my side: do not be faithless, but believing.' Thomas answered him, 'My Lord and my God!' Jesus said unto him, 'Have you believed because you have seen me? Blessed are those who have not seen and yet believe.' "

The story of the Ascension is told by Luke, both in the Gospel and in the first chapter of the Book of Acts. The account as given in Acts is more in detail. Jesus met with his disciples in Jerusalem, according to the story in Acts, and gave them a few final words of encouragement. No identification of the place is given as to where the Ascension took place. We simply are told, "As they were looking on, he was lifted up, and a cloud took him out of their sight. And while they were gazing into heaven as he went, behold, two men stood by them in white robes, and said, 'Men of Galilee, why do you stand looking into heaven? This Jesus, who was taken up from you into heaven, will come in the same manner as you saw him go into heaven.' " Around this text is built the belief held by millions of Christians known as "the second coming."

The Gospel accounts of this period contain other psychic events which should be mentioned. Matthew, for instance, relates this story: "And the graves were opened; and many bodies of the saints which slept arose, and came out of their graves after his resurrection, and went into the holy city, and appeared unto many." (Matthew 27:52-53)

Later, in Acts, we read: "And when the day of Pentecost was fully come, they were all with one accord in one place. And suddenly there came a sound from heaven as of a rushing mighty wind, and it filled the house where they were sitting. And there appeared unto them cloven tongues like as of fire, and it sat upon each of them. And they were filled with the Holy Spirit, and began to speak with other tongues, as the Spirit gave them utterance." (Acts 2:1-4)

Other passages might have been included in this study of the psychic nature of the beginnings of Christianity, but these suffice for the basis of our discussion.

The fundamentalist, the Roman Catholic, and the Greek Orthodox consider these things as inspired scripture which must be accepted as a true record of what took place. The skeptic will call them idle tales or wishful thinking or hallucination. I cannot accept either viewpoint.

First of all I agree with St. Paul that the body of Jesus in which He manifested Himself to His disciples after the Resurrection was not a body of flesh and blood. "There is a natural body, and there is a spiritual body," he says. To the disciples, who knew nothing about psychical research, the appearance of Jesus would seem to be a physical body, and they would speak of it as just that. In this I am sure they were mistaken. It was His astral body that survived the death of the physical body and it was in this astral body that Jesus manifested Himself after His death. Take for example the time when He appeared in a room "the door being closed."

Now flesh and bones do not pass through wooden doors, but an astral body can pass through such a door as easily as I can pass through fog. And although doubting Thomas demanded that he put his finger into the nail prints, there is no indication that he did so. In fact in John 20:17 we read, when Mary meets Jesus; "Jesus saith unto her, 'Touch me not: for I am not yet ascended to my Father.' "

Also we note that in the garden Mary did not recognize Jesus, but "supposed him to be the gardener." Neither did the two on the road to Emmaus recognize Jesus till he broke the bread and blessed it. If these are true psychic experiences we can account for this inability to recognize Jesus because they saw His astral body rather than His former physical body.

In the second place the Resurrection of Jesus does not stand by itself as a separate event in history. As St. Paul says, "If there be no resurrection of the dead, then is Christ not risen: For if the dead rise not, then is not Christ raised: and if Christ be not raised, your faith is vain." (I Corinthians 15:13-16 and 17) This indicates that to St. Paul resurrection was part of God's eternal purpose and plan for the souls of His children. Paul was convinced that Jesus—the same Jesus who had been crucified on the cross and had died and been laid in a tomb—had risen and been seen not only in his own experience on the road to Damascus but by his disciples and by many others in the Christian group.

Here seems to me indisputable evidence of the *reality* of the experience, an experience of "seeing" Jesus, risen after the death of His physical body. It is difficult to understand the triumphant faith and amazing courage these early followers of Jesus suddenly revealed, after such despondency and grief as followed the Crucifixion, unless we accept the witness they give of a *risen Lord*. Nor is it possible to explain the past two thousand years of the history of the Christian Church, with all its faults, apart from faith in resurrection.

We do not, it seems to me, need to accept the disciples' interpretation of the Resurrection. To them it was a resurrected, transformed, physical body. It is fair to add that this does not seem to have been St. Paul's interpretation. For him it was a spritiual personality, not a physical body, that claimed their love and loyalty.

Without belief in a spiritual world, religion loses all meaning. If bodily death ends the existence of all consciousness, then the only ultimate reality is this material world itself. It is impossible for me to accept this hypothesis of man and the universe.

My own steadfast conviction, based on years of study in the field of psychical research, is this: I believe that Jesus Christ was crucified and did die physically. Later He was able to manifest to His disciples that He was still alive and would remain a living Christ.

It is not important or necessary to accept all the interpretations of the Gospel writers as to the events on that first Easter. Psychical research has opened new doors of understanding of these phenomena. Back of the manifestations there was, I believe, *a cause; and for me that cause was Jesus Himself*. Telepathy and clairvoyance undoubtedly are factors in the experiences of the disciples. It seems to me that disproof of this is beyond scientific demonstration. As Dr. Horace Westwood writes, "It can never be proved, except on moral grounds, that Jesus conquered death. In the light of modern psychic research, it is well within the bounds of probability that the Resurrection faith owed its origin to those types of phenomena for which, in my judgment, the evidence is indisputable."

Psychical research has given me a larger faith, not one based on unproved and incomprehensible dogmas but one justified by scientific research. I am able to affirm belief in a spiritual world and in the survival of the spirit as an evolutionary process in which progress and increasing knowledge are the rewards, rather than golden harps and crowns.

I believe that in "Him we live and move and have our being," and in Jesus and His Resurrection I find an expression of God's will and purpose. For He is the God not of the dead but of the living.

19

This I Believe

I sit here now on the shaded porch of our quiet island home, and I summarize. An arm's length away is the sprawling bed of English ivy grown from a slip from Warwickshire. A hundred feet below is the calm lagoon, and now a herring gull drops a clam to the rocks below and sweeps down to peck its lunch from the shattered shell.

Although I cannot hear it a great swept-wing jet arcs high above me; I see its contrails in the sky. The wind upturns the limbs of spruce we planted twenty years ago, and behind me in the kitchen the refrigerator hums. Marion, my wife for over forty years, sits writing at the table.

This is the life I have known for more than seven decades; it is solid, comforting, understandable, familiar. It is secure because it is these things; it makes sense because we know it. And as I sit in convex tubing on webs of woven nylon conjured out of chemicals I am struck with nagging thoughts. Is not a seagull only a seagull, and a clamshell made of calcium? Is not a jet bomber merely the steel and plastic and electronic results of the laws of aerodynamics? Is not English ivy a pretty plant—and nothing more? Are all these things just that—and nothing more?

Am I being—have I been—somewhat ludicrous about the psychic? I am in a world of turbines, neutrons, internal combustion, and quantum mathematics, yet I talk of Shanti Devi. As I write of "talking" horses and proxy sittings and Dr. Rush and flying ash trays do I subject myself to scorn?

Why cannot I see *only* the feathered herring gull and think *only* in terms of calcium for shattered clamshells? Why? Why does the other-phase, the other-life, the other-fact intrigue and occupy my mind? Why cannot I be content with merely what I see? What do I believe?

Am I convinced that I shall still be able to think, to remember, to know, when my physical brain turns to dust? Am I sure of immortality?

I wish that I could say without reservation that I am sure; that the message of the risen Christ is so real, so true, so genuine that it leaves no single doubt as to immortality. But my intellect does not permit me to make such an affirmation. I still have doubts. I still have questions that never will be answered in my earthly life—perhaps never.

And yet there are things I can affirm. I believe in God, a living God, just, merciful, loving, revealed in countless prophets and saints and in the life and message of Jesus Christ. I have faith in God. At times my belief in immortality grows weak, my vision dim; but not my faith in Him. Because He has never failed me in my earthly life I believe that He will be with me in the valley of the shadow of death.

My earthly life has been a good one. My wife and I have known anxious hours and sickness, and we have lived through massacres in Turkey, two terrible World Wars, but so far as we are concerned we can say that God has been good to us. If the grave is to be the end, our lives still have been worth the living. But it is not our lives that are involved in this question, it is the character of the God we have trusted that is involved.

If life *ends* in the grave rather than dawning immortal *through* the grave, then there is no such God as I have loved. In this case Jesus was only a mistaken Galilean peasant carpenter, beautiful in His life, with a glowing message and vision for mankind, but mistaken in His central conviction as to the meaning of life and the kind of God He spoke of as "our Heavenly Father."

So, while I have spoken of my doubts, let me speak of my faith, for my faith far outshines my clouds of doubt. So, were you to ask me, do I believe in immortality, I would say with conviction: Yes, in spite of my doubts, in spite of my questionings; yes, I do believe.

What is it now that I believe? I have said that I believe in God and in the kind of God who manifested Himself in Jesus of Nazareth. In a way James Martineau, the great English theologian, was right when he said, "We do not believe in immortality because we have proved it, but we forever try to prove it because we believe in it."

I find it no greater a mystery to believe that we shall live in another body after this present life than to believe that I have been born into this body and lived on earth. Both are mysteries beyond man's ability to fathom. In college classrooms across the land we teach that life evolved from a single cell; that from this cell evolved not only prehistoric man but the great philosophers of Greece, the prophets of Israel, men named Jesus, Milton, and Einstein. Yet who can prove this with certainty of knowledge? It remains a mystery. But we live as though it were true and we teach it.

Man seems to be made on the scale of two worlds, the one temporal and fleeting, the other eternal and abiding. Man has all the potentiality for continuing after the death of the physical body; he has so much left when he leaves this earth. It was Victor Hugo who wrote: "For half a century I have been writing my thoughts in prose and verse, but, now that I am dying, I feel that I have not said one one-thousandth part of what is in me." When John Adams was a very old man, near the close of his earthly life, a friend asked him one day, "And how are you today, Mr. Adams?" To which he replied, "This physical house in which I live is wearing out, but John Adams was never more alive."

Few of us do not feel within us potentialities that can never be fulfilled in this life. As the great painter Corot wrote in his old age, "If the Lord lets me live two years longer, I think I can paint something beautiful." The sense of incompleteness and often of frustration caused by the brevity of our earthly lives or by the limitations of our environment increases as we enter the last period of our pilgrimage here on earth.

And I believe that the whole evolutionary process leads us to the rational conclusion that the Creator plans that man shall become a more perfect being than is possible amid the limitations and frustrations that beset so many here on earth. I believe that what science tells us about the indestructibility of energy is only the physical equivalent of what religion affirms about the immortality of the personality.

Now I find this belief in immortality universal. As Ralph Waldo Emerson wrote, "Here is this wonderful thought: Wherever man ripens, the audacious belief in immortality presently appears. As soon as thought is exercised, this belief is inevitable. Whence came it? Who put it into the mind of man?"

David Livingstone in his diary tells of coming one evening on a group of primitive savages in a jungle of Africa, sitting around a campfire. And they, like men of all cultures and times, were engaged in a serious discussion of the questions, "Whence did we come? Why are we here? Where do we go?"

When we read the agnostics something within us protests. Clarence Darrow once said, "No life is of much value, and every death is but a little loss. The most satisfactory part of life is the time spent in sleep, when one is utterly oblivious to existence." When I first read that statement of Darrow's during the days of my early ministry I thought, "His own efforts on behalf of those in need, and his pursuit of truth, belie his words." But what empty cynical words they are.

Let me affirm some of the things I do believe.

I believe that we do not *have* souls but that we *are* souls. For a few short years we inhabit these bodies of flesh and bones. But our real selves are not material. In hospitals I have seen men who had lost arms, legs, and other parts of their physical selves, but they were as alert, as conscious, as vivid personalities as before this loss. In cases where the physical brain had been injured, the personality was unable to function, but I am convinced that only the physical brain was injured, not the spirit personality. For me the astral body is the real body that survivies death. This astral body is the one St. Paul refers to when he says "...there is a natural body and there is a celestial body" (I Corinthians 15:40) or, "For flesh and blood cannot inherit eternal life" (I Corinthians 15:50) or, "For this corruption shall put on incorruption, and this mortal shall put on immortality" (I Corinthians 15:53).

When we die our astral self leaves the physical body and is no longer limited by time and space as we are when in the flesh. Already I experience this freedom to a certain degree. Sitting here I close my eyes and in an instant I find myself on the Acropolis at Athens. The Parthenon and the city below stand out in clear and sharp outline, more real, more stimulating to my mind than the room in which I am sitting. Only my physical limitations prevent me from *being* on the Acropolis. Or in another second I can be in Agra sitting on that marble seat in front of the Taj Mahal, where my wife and I once sat in the moonlight. Again I feel the thrilling beauty of that shrine. But my physical limitations will not permit me to cover the miles to India.

Time and space have a far different meaning for us than they had for our grandparents. How absurd to them would be the assertion that one could have breakfast in London and luncheon in New York! For the pioneers crossing the country in covered wagons how impossible it would have been to *believe* that their children's children would fly through the air from New York to California in a few hours!

It seems to me no more difficult to believe that there lies before us another world of life and color and sound than to believe that this present world should exist and we be born into it, capable of enjoying sight and hearing and feeling.

My belief as to the nature of that other world is based on many "communications." It seems to me beyond dispute that thought can be transmitted from mind to mind by means now unknown to science.

Just so, I believe that thoughts can and have been transmitted from minds in that other world to minds in ours. What do they tell us about the world in which they live? If God is the Creator of this world we know something of His desires and ways of expressing those desires. He must love color, harmony, beauty. A garden, a green lawn, a flashing sea, a snow-clad mountain, a quiet valley, and a brook are but a few of His expressions of His spirit. We are able to tell a painting, a marble form, a symphony, by the style of the artist; each has a personal and significant way of expressing himself. Now, if the creator of our world reveals to us His love of color, of gardens, of singing brooks and sunlit seas, then it is rational to suppose that in just such a manner does He manifest His creative power in other worlds and for other spirits. "In my Father's house are many mansions." (John 14:2)

Materialistic science has had its day. That day is gone. The worship of materialism is coming to an end and a new and intense interest in nonmaterial concepts is dawning on mankind. Dr. Leslie Weatherhead, the well-known British writer and theologian, has written, "I venture to prophecy that the road of man's intellectual progress will soon take a turning leading through the difficult and hilly country vaguely called 'psychical research.' "

At Harvard Professor James once said something that made a deep impression on me, "The death of the body may be the end of the sensational use of the mind, but only the beginning of its intellectual use."

Yes, I believe, in spite of those doubts with which my mind struggles, and probably always will struggle in this world. I still believe in immortality.

COMPLETE MEDITATION

Steve Kravette

Complete Meditation presents a broad range of metaphysical concepts and
meditation techniques in the same direct, easy-to-assimilate style of the
author's best-selling *Complete Relaxation*. Personal experience is the teacher
and this unique book is your guide. The free, poetic format leads you
through a series of exercises that build on each other, starting with breathing
patterns, visualization exercises and a growing confidence that meditation is
easy and pleasurable. Graceful illustrations flow along with the text.

    Complete Meditation is for readers at all levels of experience. It makes
advanced metaphysics and esoteric practices accessible without years of study
of the literature, attachment to gurus or initiation into secret societies.
Everyone can meditate, everyone is psychic, and with only a little attention
everyone can bring oneself and one's circumstances into harmony.

    Experienced meditators will appreciate the more advanced techniques,
including more sophisticated breathing patterns, astral travel, past-life
regression, and much more. All readers will appreciate being shown how
ordinarily "boring" experiences are really illuminating gateways into the
complete meditation experience. Whether you do all the exercises or not, just
reading this book is a pleasure.

    Complete meditation can happen anywhere, any time, in thousands of
different ways. A candle flame, a daydream, music, sex, a glint of light on
your ring. In virtually any circumstances. *Complete Meditation* shows you
how.

ISBN 0-914918-28-1
320 pages, 6½" x 9¼", paper,

$9.95

BIRTHDAY NUMEROLOGY

by Dusty Bunker and Victoria Knowles

One of the unique things about you is the day on which you were born. In *Birthday Numerology*, well-known numerologist Dusty Bunker and psychic counselor Victoria Knowles combine their knowledge of numerology, symbolism and psychic development to present a clear and coherent presentation of how the day you were born affects your personality.

Unlike other methods of divination, the beauty of this book lies in its simple and direct presentation of the meaning behind personal numbers. Rather than having to perform complicated calculations, all you need to do is know your birthday. The book is uncannily accurate, written in a warm and engaging style and, above all, is easy to use.

The introductory chapters discuss the foundation and validity of numerology and will help you discover why the date of your birth is crucial in determining your personality. From there, *Birthday Numerology* examines the traits and characteristics inherent in people born on each day of the month.

Dusty Bunker and Vikki Knowles have written a book that is much more than just a delineation of various personalities, it is truly a guidebook to your journey through the 31 days.

ISBN 0-914918-39-7

225 pages, 6½"x 9¼", paper

$9.95

DEVELOP YOUR PSYCHIC SKILLS

Enid Hoffman

Psychic skills are as natural to human beings as walking and talking and are much more easily learned. Here are the simple directions *and* the inside secrets from noted teacher and author Enid Hoffman.

Develop Your Psychic Skills gives you a broad overview of the whole field of psychic experiences. The exercises and practices given in this book are enjoyable and easy to do. Use them to strengthen and focus your own natural abilities and turn them into precise, coordinated skills. You'll be amazed at the changes that begin to happen in your life as you activate the right hemisphere of your brain, the intuitive, creative, psychic half, which has been ignored for so long.

This book shows you how your natural psychic powers can transform your life when you awaken the other half of your brain. It teaches you techniques for knowing what others are doing, feeling and thinking. You can see what the future holds and explore past lives. You can learn to locate lost objects and people. You can become a psychic healer. It is all open to you.

Develop occasional hunches into definite foreknowledge. Sharpen wandering fantasies and daydreams into clear and accurate pictures of events in other times and places. Choose what you want to do with your life by developing your psychic skills. When you finish this book you'll realize, as thousands of others have using Enid Hoffman's techniques, that the day you began to develop your psychic skills was the day you began to become fully conscious, fully creative and fully alive.

ISBN 0-914918-29-X
192 pages, 6½" x 9¼", paper, $7.95

ORDER FROM: Para Research, Dept. LD, Rockport, MA 01966. Add .50 per book postage.